Principles of style
for the business writer

Principles of style for the business writer

William C. Paxson

DODD, MEAD & COMPANY

NEW YORK

Grateful acknowledgment is made to use the following material:

Excerpt from *The Lazlo Letters* © 1977 by Don Novello. Workman Publishing, New York. Reprinted with permission of the publisher. Excerpt from *Zen and the Art of Motorcycle Maintenance* by Robert M. Pirsig. Copyright © 1974 by Robert M. Pirsig. By permission of William Morrow and Company. Excerpt from *The Language of the Law* by David Melinkoff. Little, Brown and Co., 1963. Reprinted by permission of the publishers. Excerpt from *Simply Stated*, the monthly newsletter of the Document Design Center, No. 32, December 1982–January 1983. Used by permission. Excerpt from *Child Care Initiatives for Working Parents: Why Employers Get Involved*, an AMA Survey Report, by Renee Y. Magid, pp. 9–11, 14. © 1983 AMA Membership Publications Division, American Management Associations, New York. All rights reserved. Used by permission of the publisher. Excerpt from *No More Secondhand God* by R. Buckminster Fuller. (Southern Illinois University Press, 1963). Reprinted by permission of The Buckminster Fuller Institute, 1743 S. La Cienega Blvd., Los Angeles, CA 90035.

Published by Dodd, Mead & Company, Inc.
79 Madison Avenue, New York, N.Y. 10016
Distributed in Canada by
McClelland and Stewart Limited, Toronto
Manufactured in the United States of America
Designed by Kay Lee
First Edition

Library of Congress Cataloging in Publication Data

Paxson, William C.
  Principles of style for the business writer.

  Bibliography: p.
  Includes index.
  1. English language—Rhetoric. 2. English language—
Style. 3. English language—Business English. I. Title.
PE1479.B87P39 1985   808′.066651   85-4401
ISBN 0-396-08725-6
ISBN 0-396-08734-5 (pbk.)

Contents

Introduction

I believe that the best way to introduce the book is to say a few words about three terms in the title: *Business Writer, Style,* and *Principles.*

Business writer. In times past, the business writer was the entrepreneur or the correspondence secretary. Today the business writer is the manager, the systems analyst, the engineer, the government official, the economist, the scientist, the personnel specialist—or any of a number of other occupations. These are the people doing the bulk of the writing nowadays, not journalists or novelists.

Style. Consider the definition of style offered by E. B. White. In a long and distinguished career, White served as one of the original staff writers on *The New Yorker* magazine, wrote *Charlotte's Web* and *Stuart Little* plus many fine essays, and was coauthor of *The Elements of Style*—a concise treatise on good writing that has sold more than two million copies. In recognition of his contributions to American writing, White was awarded a special Pulitzer Prize in 1978.

In *The Elements of Style,* White says: "There is no satisfactory explanation of style, no infallible guide to good writing, no assurance that a person who thinks clearly will be able to write clearly, no key that unlocks the door, no inflexible rule by which the young writer may shape his course."[1]

The Elements of Style is the modern classic in the field. It begins with advice on how to use the apostrophe, covers word usage and grammar, and ends with a brief but highly literary essay on the writer's responsibilities. In centuries past, the teaching of style was more general. "Study the great writers," the master would say, "and emulate them."

In this book, the teaching is not general at all. Numerous samples and explanations cover specific instances that the writer meets daily on the job. Word usage is of prime importance, and that subject is given considerable treatment early in the book. Later chapters deal with sentences and paragraphs, and chapters toward the end are on arranging whole pieces of writing. Clarity and brevity are stressed, as is the need to write for the reader. Grammar is, admittedly, treated only lightly, for this is not a grammar book but is instead a book on how to write solid, lucid business prose.

Principles. Chapter titles are stated as principles and sound like terse, direct orders: "Be Specific"; "Rewrite, Rewrite, Rewrite." I have used this style for emphasis, in hopes that readers will find it easy to remember the principles. They are principles, however, not commandments, laws, or rules. If something can be written in a better way than I have described, the principles should be improved upon, adapted, stretched, bent, or violated outright.

The principles are derived from my experiences as a writer and editor over almost two decades. During those years, I have conducted employee training in business and technical writing, and I have worked as a self-employed editor and writer and have performed that same kind of work in government. I have never taught on a college campus, and I have never worked for a newspaper, book, or magazine publisher. All of my experience has been gained while doing, on a daily basis, the types of writing described in this book. In an era dominated by business and scientific communication, this experience is of greater value to you than it would be had I gained it elsewhere.

Finally, the word *style* is infrequently used in the book. This is as it should be, for the writer of a cookbook would bore readers to tears if the word *cook* appeared in every recipe. Nevertheless, the subject here is style.

Principles of style
for the business writer

Care for your reader

1

Advice on caring for your reader, adding the personal touch, the hidden message (metacommunications), and how not to insult readers. *Plus* comments and lessons from comedian Don Novello and novelists Kurt Vonnegut and Morris L. West.

Novelist Kurt Vonnegut is best known for books such as *Slaughterhouse Five* and *Cat's Cradle.* Vonnegut also appeared in one of the commendable series of advertisements that the International Paper Company published on the importance of the printed word. The Royal Bank of Canada thought enough of Vonnegut's remarks in that ad to reprint them in its prestigious newsletter, *The Royal Bank Letter.* Vonnegut's words will serve as an excellent introduction to this chapter:

> Why should you examine your writing style with the idea of improving it? Do so as a mark of respect for your readers. If you scribble your thoughts any which way, your readers will surely feel that you care nothing for them.[1]

We do care for our readers, for the most fundamental reason of all: We are humans. We like to care for others, and we like others to care for us. Caring feels good, as simple as that sounds. We also care for our readers because of the reasons shown in the letters of Lazlo Toth.

THE LAZLO LETTERS

Lazlo Toth was the creation of comedian Don Novello, better known as television's Father Guido Sarducci, the Vatican gossip columnist.

The Toth-Novello character was sincere, semi-informed, and somewhat of a lunatic. Over a period of several years in the mid-1970s, he wrote ludicrous letters to world leaders, politicians, and corporate executives—and they frequently wrote back.

For instance, Lazlo Toth became concerned about what jelly had to do with an **Egg McMuffin**. He expressed his concerns to Ray Kroc, McDonald's chief executive:

Dear Mr. Kroc,

Recently I was driving to Pasadena, California, and I saw a billboard for McDonald's that made me start thinking. It showed an egg McMuffin, which looked very good, and next to it there was some jelly.

Personally, I think a lot of people will not like the egg McMuffin with jelly. It would be like putting jelly on top of eggs!

I think that billboard will make a lot of people not order an egg McMuffin—even though I know they don't have to use the jelly if they don't want to.

It just makes me sad that the egg McMuffin looked so good and that jelly just goes and spoils the whole thing.

I write this just as a suggestion since I have enjoyed your hamburgers and fries so much and I would hate to

*see your fine organization be hurt by trying to be nice
and giving out jelly, but it just doesn't go.*

Sincerely,
Lazlo Toth

McDonald's replied:

Dear Mr. Toth:

*In our Egg McMuffin outdoor billboards we show jelly
next to our newest product for one main reason—we have
found that a lot of our customers take off the top half of
the muffin and eat it separately from the rest of our Egg
McMuffin product. The jelly is provided to make the top
half, when eaten separately, taste even better.*

*And, just in case you haven't tried an Egg McMuffin
yet, here's a gift certificate which should go most of the
way to buy you one at your nearby McDonald's. (We
think you'll find it delicious.) Or, you can use it to buy
anything else you might prefer.*

*Many thanks for your letter to Mr. Kroc—and thank
you for your continued patronage.*

Sincerely,
McDONALD'S SYSTEM, INC.
Darrough Diamond
National Advertising Manager

As if this exchange wasn't too farfetched, Lazlo Toth
wrote again. This time he complained that he wanted to
put jelly on a McDonald's hamburger, but McDonald's
wouldn't give him any jelly. Patiently, the McDonald's
correspondent explained that few people like hamburgers
that way and thanked Lazlo Toth for his note.

Novello compiled dozens of similar letters and replies in a book, *The Lazlo Letters.*[2] Bookstores shelve *The Lazlo Letters* under "Humor," and it *is* funny.

It is also an excellent lesson in the importance of business correspondence, for Toth-Novello received a reply in almost every case. The replies were well-written and followed the principles of good grammar, punctuation, and capitalization. Moreover, the content of the replies shows that companies did not treat Lazlo Toth's complaints as petty or unworthy of consideration. The cost of answering was more than outweighed by the risk of losing a customer, even though the customer almost seemed to be having fun at the company's expense. Overall, customer satisfaction was the most important consideration. These writers cared for their readers!

ADDING THE PERSONAL TOUCH

Research shows that readers understand and remember passages when the writing is on personal terms.[3] Writing can be made to sound personal by using pronouns such as *you* and *we* and by featuring people in the writing.

The "you" approach. Advertising writers know this trick well. Their writing is directed to *you*, not "to the reader." "*You* can have beautiful skin." "Now *you* can afford the house of *your* dreams." "How *you* can earn $50,000 a year for the rest of *your* life."

Letter writers take the same approach. They use *you* and *your* to appeal to the reader and to draw the reader into the letter. "Thank *you* for *your* letter of . . ." and "In *your* letter of March 24, *you* mentioned . . . " are typical beginnings that add the personal touch to writing.

The personal touch of the "you" approach has other applications. As an example, note the improvement when the word *investor* as used in this sample from a mutual fund brochure—

> The funds accrue net investment income daily as dividends and distribute it quarterly to *investors* as a dividend or a reinvestment in additional shares. It is an *investor* decision. If there are capital gains, they will be distributed annually. Again, *investors* may request a check for these funds or reinvest them automatically.

—is changed to *you:*

> The funds accrue net investment income daily as dividends and distribute it quarterly to *you* as a dividend or a reinvestment in additional shares. It is *your* decision. If there are capital gains, they will be distributed annually. Again, *you* may request . . .

The change makes the writing more personal, more direct, and more appealing.

The "you" approach can also be used when writing policies, directives, rules, or regulations. Here is a pair of before-and-after samples from the Housing and Urban Development Privacy Act Regulations. As often happens when regulations are rewritten, the system of numbering and headings has been changed.

Before

(d) The requirements for identification of individuals seeking access to records are as follows:

(1) *In person.* Each individual making a request in person shall be required to present satisfactory proof of identity. The means of proof, in the order of preference and priority, are:

(i) A document bearing the individual's photograph

(ii) A document bearing the individual's signature

After

16.7 Proof of identity.

(a) This section tells *you* what *you* have to do to prove *your* identity when making a request.

(b) When *you* make a request in person—

(1) *You* should show the Privacy Act Officer a document with *your* photograph or signature on it.[4]

Again, the personal touch makes the writing considerably more readable.

Where are the people? Many business topics are concerned with the activities of people. Yet all too often, the people do not appear, as is the case with this sample:

> We are not dealing with little robots. We are interacting with capable aware processors of information, so long as the inputs are simple enough to be grasped.[5]

The words are those of a businessman. His message is not "simple enough to be grasped," unless you know that "capable aware processors of information" are little children and that the "inputs" are television commercials. By wallowing in this cold, impersonal style he is speaking of children as if they are indeed little robots. If he uses words this way, how does he think? In his mind, are children not children but just little robots? Does he *care* about children?

Too many writers treat readers as things other than people. Educationists talk of schoolchildren as *subsystems*. The scientist changes pregnant women to *gravidae*. People participating in laboratory research are called *elements* or *subjects.* Parking lot operators call their clients *parkers.* Job descriptions refer to *incumbents,* and directives and rules often speak of *operators* and *users.* And of course there is the formal *one: "One* should mail this certificate in by June 30 so as to prevent . . ."

That kind of writing is coldhearted. It turns people off. It makes the reader say, Why doesn't the writer acknowledge that people exist? Doesn't the writer care about people?

More than likely, the writer does care about people. Scientific objectivity or timidity, however, are blocks that prevent the writer from dealing with the topic in human terms. Thus we see items like this:

> Family A consists of six subjects. The family's annual income is $32,000, which is well above the poverty level. Nevertheless, the members of Family A do not have everything they want. To take but one example, the head of the household would like to buy a new set of golf clubs.

Family A can be made to sound more flesh-and-blood by giving them names. When this is done, common, popular names are used to avoid the possibility of singling out one family. The technique makes the topic more readable, with no loss of scientific objectivity. And the slightly stilted language in the sample above can be simplified too:

> The Smith family of six with a $32,000-a-year income isn't poor. Nevertheless, they don't have everything they want. To take but one example, Sam Smith would like to buy a new set of golf clubs.

Don't write "whodunits." It helps to let readers know from time to time that someone actually wrote the piece. That is, the use of first-person pronouns such as *I, me, myself, we,* and *us* can go a long way toward humanizing writing.

These first-person pronouns add a lot to letters and to writing like this.

Before

The top part of the statement will be used to process the payment to your account, and its enclosure in the envelope supplied will aid in the accurate crediting of your account.

After

We will use the top portion of your statement to process the payment to your account. If you enclose it in the envelope that *we* supplied with the bill, *we* will be better able to credit your account accurately.

Some writers avoid writing in the first person for fear of sounding immodest, of using too many *I*'s. That is a realistic and practical apprehension. It can be avoided by remembering that once you've established who's writing, it's not necessary to keep reminding the reader. The first sample below shows an overuse of the first person. Note how the second sample carries the same message, with the same degree of first-person authority, but with fewer pronouns:

Immodest

I have reviewed the plan and offer these comments. *I* see no need to develop additional goals for Division A for the coming fiscal year. In *my* opinion, the number of newly assigned projects does not warrant added goals. Furthermore, *I* see no way to achieve any added goals unless funding is increased.

Modest

I have reviewed the plan and offer these comments. No need exists to develop additional goals for Division A for the coming fiscal year, for the number of newly assigned projects does not warrant added goals. Furthermore, there is no way to achieve any added goals unless funding is increased.

THE HIDDEN MESSAGE

In caring for our readers, we should keep in mind that writing sends two messages—the obvious one and the hidden one. The obvious message is the one directly expressed in words. The hidden message is expressed some other way, as in a misspelling or a mistake in grammar. This hidden message is known as a *metacommunication.*

The study of metacommunications is in its infancy, and it is far too early to make definite, bold statements. In fact, only one report of research can be cited here.[6] Still, this little research does give us some hint as to how readers react to the hidden message. As examples:

Trite expressions	*Metacommunication*
Have a nice day.	I do not have time to think of a better close.
If we can help you in any other way, please let us know.	You're nothing special to me; I use the same courteous close for all my letters.

Spelling errors

I *agre.*

This *sould* reflect on your March statement.

Metacommunication

My busy schedule does not permit such a trivial matter as checking the spelling of a word.

I do not take time to proofread my letters.

Grammatical error

There are [plural] always a *possibility* [singular] that we will reinstate such a publication, but at the moment I can't say when.

Metacommunication

I am not very good at making nouns and verbs agree.

It is only a short step from these metacommunications to readers saying, "Well, if you really cared, you wouldn't have made such a mistake." In other words, little things mean a lot.

A LESSON FROM THE BUREAUCRACY

One of the things government agencies must do is publish public hearing notices. One purpose of these notices is to inform people of proposed actions. Another purpose is to solicit public opinion. These notices are printed in newspapers and sometimes distributed as letters. A typical public notice begins as this one does, worded very bureaucratically and impersonally:

NOTICE IS HEREBY GIVEN that the Executive Officer of the [organizational name deleted], or by his delegate, pursuant to the authority vested by Sections 39000, 39001, 39003, 39500, 39515, 39516, 39600, 39602, 39605, and 41500 of the Health and Safety Code, and pursuant to a delegation made October 22, 1981, will hold a public meeting, at the time and place set forth below, to consider a suggested control measure to reduce fugitive emissions of photochemically reactive organic compounds from pressure relief valves in petroleum refineries. . . .

One state agency in California grew weary of that style of writing and changed to this form:

Dear Citizen:

On October 13 Governor Brown directed the Department of Health Services to begin phasing out the land disposal of certain toxic wastes. The Executive Order applies to both off-site and on-site land disposal, and represents a radical shift away from the use of land disposal facilities for any and all types of hazardous wastes. The Executive Order also commits the State to encouraging the construction of environmentally sound facilities for recycling, treatment, and destruction of those hazardous wastes diverted from land disposal.

The purpose of the enclosed discussion paper is to solicit your comments concerning the implementation of the Governor's Executive Order. The discussion paper identifies the types of wastes that will be considered for phase-out from land disposal, concentration limits, and the target dates for the phase-out. It also outlines our proposed approach to extensions to the phase-out dates if alternative technologies are not available. . . .

It sounds a lot nicer, a lot more human.

HOW TO INSULT READERS

It is all too easy to pour word after word upon a piece of paper and say nothing. When that happens, readers become impatient and insulted.

As a case in point, consider this long-winded paragraph. The sentences are numbered for later reference.

(1) In preparing this overview, our goal goes beyond fulfilling a narrow mandate. (2) In fact, this overview is one part of a larger, ongoing process of policy research and implementation aimed at effectuating many of the enormously complex solutions that could not possibly be handled in a single document. (3) This document is a starting point for a series of hearings, workshops, and seminars in which our proposals will be refined through open discussions with persons in the public and private sectors who represent various interests. (4) By July of 1984 we intend to publish the state's energy contingency plan. (5) In addition, the [organizational name deleted] has let a series of contracts for the purpose of studying over the next two years some of the more difficult policy issues that we have identified as needing further analysis, and that cannot realistically be resolved in a shorter time. (6) In the broadest view, the intended outcome of this entire process is, ultimately, a stable economic and social environment in which energy availability and prices are less ubiquitous concerns. (7) In this context, the meaning of the combined visual/verbal image on the cover of this document becomes more evident. (8) What is a more poignant symbol of this society's energy vulnerability than the daily highway commuter? (9) And what is more desirable than

reaching energy security? (10) The purpose of this document is to make sure we are moving in the right direction.

The faults of this paragraph can be grouped into these categories:

Overstatement and misstatement. The writer goes "beyond fulfilling a narrow mandate" (1) to "enormously complex solutions that could not possibly be handled in a single document" (2). "Open discussions" will be held with "persons in the public and private sectors who represent various interests" (3). There. All bases are touched, even if we ask: Is there such a thing as a closed discussion, and with whom or what else would we hold discussions other than persons?

In addition, some "policy issues" are so difficult that the organization is paying people to study these issues for two years (5). *Study* for two years, mind you, not act on them. The writer takes "the broadest view" of "this entire process" (6) and ends by saying, "The purpose of this document is to make sure we are moving in the right direction" (10). Certainly the organization would not want to move us in the wrong direction.

Confusion of purpose. The document being discussed is only an "overview" (1 and 2). Or is it a "starting point" (3)?

Waffling and hedging. "We *intend* to publish" (4), "the *purpose* of studying," which is saying the studies may not come about, and "needing *further* analysis" (5), and *"intended* outcome" (6).

Empty buzz words and bureaucratic clichés. "Fulfilling a narrow mandate" (1), "ongoing process" and "policy research and implementation" (2), and "policy issues" (5).

Misused words. "What is a more *poignant* symbol of this society's energy vulnerability than the daily highway commuter?" (8). When it comes to energy vulnerability, a *poignant* (emotionally moving) symbol might be the family shivering in a shack in Maine, but the daily highway commuter deserves some lesser modifier such as *frequently seen, everyday, common,* or *recurrent.* "And what is more *desirable* than reaching energy security?" (9). Careful usage tells us the answer: Someone of the opposite sex may be more *desirable,* but energy security is more *important.* The "combined visual/verbal image" (7) is merely an *illustration.* The word *goal* (1) is misused, as is *fact* (2). A goal is stationary and "goes" nowhere, and the statement made in sentence (2) is not a fact but an assertion.

Overall, there are a lot of words in that paragraph—but what value are they to the reader? How does that paragraph help anyone do anything?

Empty prose like that is easy to turn out, and the way to avoid doing so is to ask yourself: What does my reader NEED to know?

Notice where the emphasis is, on the word *need.* Good writing is not the act of spewing out words the writer feels compelled to get rid of. Instead, good writing is looking at things from the reader's point of view and working to satisfy the reader's *needs.* The paragraph we've just read does nothing to satisfy the reader's needs and is a waste of time and money and an insult overall.

We began this chapter with a quote from Kurt Vonnegut on caring for your reader. Let's close in the same manner, with a quote from Morris L. West, author of several best-selling books (*The Shoes of the Fisherman; The Devil's Advocate*):

Writing is like making love. You have to practice to be good at it. Like the best lovemaking, it has to be done in private and with great consideration for your partner in the enterprise, who in this case is the reader.[7]

Treat words and meanings with respect

2

Advice on the many meanings of
words, clichés and *ize* endings,
the loose use of words, the
limitations of a dictionary, making
context work for you, and word
order and meaning. *Plus* the story
of a word that changed the world
and a lesson (?) about meaning
as taught by a computer.

A man who is an admiral and a prime minister, a leader
of men and a nation, ought to have command of his language. After all, words are mere things to be used as one
wants, not independent creatures, like people, with
minds of their own.

For one brief moment, such a man was not in command
of his language, and because of his mistake with one
word, the world has been changed to an extent we will
never be able to estimate.

The man was Admiral Baron Kantaro Suzuki, prime
minister of Japan from April 6 to August 16, 1945; president of the privy council and member of the *jushin* (a
body of senior statesmen); former grand chamberlain to
Emperor Hirohito; and naval hero of the Chinese-Japa-
nese and Russo-Japanese wars.

The word is *mokusatsu.* Suzuki uttered it in response

to the Potsdam Proclamation, a document calling for Japan's immediate surrender in the closing days of World War II. Suzuki later said he meant "withhold comment," the idea being to stall for time. Nevertheless, what *mokusatsu* primarily means is "kill with silence" or "ignore." Japanese translators, unable to read Suzuki's mind, translated *mokusatsu* into "ignore." The United States picked up the "ignore" meaning and reacted by dropping atomic bombs on Hiroshima and Nagasaki. The bombs ended the war, but in so doing killed more than 120,000 Japanese and plunged the world into the atomic age.[1]

The atomic age might have started anyway, then or later, regardless of the actions of Suzuki. That we don't know. But we do know from this lesson how important it is to treat words and meanings with respect.

WORDS AND MEANINGS

A word has many meanings. Semantics—the study of meaning—tells us so. So does a dictionary, and so does common sense.

For instance, suppose you stand up in a room full of people and say "chair." Everyone in the room could easily have a different mental picture of what a *chair* is: easy *chair,* recliner *chair*, lawn *chair*, beach *chair*, overstuffed *chair*, swivel *chair*, and even today's use of *chair* to mean *chair*man, *chair*woman, or *chair*person, as in "The committee *chair* called the meeting to order."

Suppose you said "bar" to a large group of people. To the lawyers in the crowd, *bar* stands for courts and judges and bailiffs and law clerks—the entire judicial system. To the mechanic in the crowd, you could be talking of nothing more complicated than a *bar* for prying.

Others in the crowd will think of a *bar* as a *bar* of soap or candy, a sand *bar*, the *bar* of a bridle, a *bar* of silver or gold, or a *bar* as a place to go for a drink.

Take the word *zero*. It's easy to think of *zero* as meaning "nothing," but we also know that *zero* is a number between the negative set of numbers and the positive set; in that respect, *zero* is something. On a graph, *zero* can be a starting point. We speak of *zero* hour not as the beginning of all time but as the starting time of a military operation such as an invasion. When talking of temperature, we use *zero* degrees Celsius, *zero* degrees Fahrenheit, and absolute *zero*. Absolute *zero* is not the number 0 but minus 273.15 degrees Celsius or minus 459.67 degrees Fahrenheit. Nothing about meaning is easy. Nothing, or is that *zero*?

Problems of meaning are compounded when the writer falls into the trap of using popular words or expressions that sound good when spoken, sometimes look good when written, but usually fail critical tests of meaning.

One such trap is the cliché. A cliché is usually criticized because it is a stale, trite expression. The most important criticism is this: What does a cliché mean? What does it mean to write "state of the art" or "state of the science"? What is "the cutting edge of technology"? "Here's where I'm coming from"? "Meaningful relationships"? "I felt comfortable with the proposal"? "The thrust of a new program"? "We verbalized our posture"? Readers deserve better. They deserve to know what the meaning is of those expressions and others like them.

Another trap is the *ize* ending. The *ize* ending has been around for almost four centuries, and nothing is wrong with ending a word in *ize* or *ing* or *ism* or any syllable for that matter, provided that is the best way to do it. Criticism of the *ize* ending seems popular these days, however, and the criticism is well-founded when the *ize* ending is used at the expense of clarity. *Prioritize* seems clear enough as a shorter way of writing *establish priorities*. The expression *localized frosts* is clear enough, except *local frosts* is shorter. The same can be said for *a personalized summary,* which could just as well be *a personal summary.* Otherwise:

finalize. "The report has been finalized." Does this mean that the report is complete or just that work on it has stopped?

optimize. "Optimize production facilities" can be read to mean "make the best use of existing production facilities" or "establish the most effective production facilities."

routinization. Are routines established? Divided into routines? Subroutines?

The loose use of words disturbs readers. Consider the word *scenario.* A *scenario* once stood for no more than an outline or synopsis of a play. Today, *scenario* is used to mean war plan, the pattern a revolution might take, or economic predictions that try to foresee the next fifty years. When used in these senses, *scenario* vastly understates the importance of these possibilities. Readers are offended by the misuse of any word, especially one so openly dishonest.

Consider also *transpire.* This word is often used today to mean "occur," as in this sentence: "These events *transpired* [occurred] after the management memo was distributed." Scientists dislike seeing *transpire* used in this manner, for the principal sense of the word pertains to the movement of vapors through tissues or pores.

And some abuses of words provide us with reason for

whimsical speculation. As an example, a sign in a doctor's office reads: "It is customary to pay for professional services when rendered." The sign does not say who's supposed to pay. Moreover, who or what is being rendered, and how—by melting over a fire? That's one meaning of the word *render*. Of course, these problems could have been avoided if the wording had been: "Please pay for professional services when they are performed."

In the face of all of the problems of meaning, what can be done?

The standard advice—use a dictionary—is good advice. A dictionary is a tool of the writing trade. A dictionary should not be left to gather dust on a shelf but should be used constantly so that it falls apart and must be replaced. Professional editors and writers often work from several dictionaries, yet many beginning writers feel that the use of a dictionary is a sign of weakness. This is unfortunate and should not be so.

To get the most out of a dictionary, you should know how a dictionary is put together. Editors of some early dictionaries operated on the theory that they could set rules for using words, that they could "freeze" language and that meanings did not change. This theory ignored the fact that languages do change. Nevertheless, the theory won out and has established the myth that a dictionary contains firm rules of meaning.

In reality, modern dictionaries are essentially history books. A dictionary editor—and there can be scores of editors working on a big dictionary—reads extensively to see how writers use words. The editor records the different usages, and these usages make up the dictionary. The editor does not dictate what a word means but simply writes down what writers take the word to mean.

This does not mean that you have carte blanche to use

words any which way. On the contrary, the best writers stay as close as possible to the traditional meaning of a word so as to avoid confusing readers. Otherwise, a dictionary does have its limitations. It reports *past* meanings and cannot foresee the future. But despite these limitations, a dictionary is still an excellent source of reference and instruction on how to use words.

You should also make *context* work for you. Context consists of the words that come before and after a word or expression. As has already been pointed out, a word can have many meanings; context can be used to help readers isolate one meaning.

An example can be made of the word *set*. The multivolume *Oxford English Dictionary* contains seventy-one *columns* of definitions for *set*. The statement "I lost two *sets*" means nothing by itself. It could stand for two *sets* of dishes or two *sets* of false teeth. But put "I lost two sets" into a letter about a tennis match, and the meaning immediately becomes clear. The surrounding words—the context—have helped to define the word *set*.

Another example of how context helps define a word is this one: "Brazil, Uruguay, and Paraguay cancelled the agreement. Argentina also abrogated the terms." The meaning of *abrogated* is explained by the words *cancelled* and *also*. Argentina *also* did something, the same as the other nations.

Otherwise, when you consider the problems—the different meanings that different people bring to a word, the limitations of a dictionary, the frailties of human understanding, the many ways to be wrong—the best thing to do is to be skeptical. Approach words and meanings with caution and treat them with respect.

WORD ORDER AND MEANING

The most inflexible principle of English usage is this: The arrangement of words in a sentence determines the meaning of that sentence. The arrangement is known as *syntax:* word order.

How important is word order? Take a look at these two groups of words:

- interest earned on investments of $17,000
- interest of $17,000 earned on investments

Both contain the same words, but the word order is different—and so is the meaning!

Playing with word order in favorite sayings can be fun. For instance, we've been told over and over again that "A penny saved is a penny earned." But is "A penny earned a penny saved"? Not necessarily. Consider "He who hesitates is lost." Can it also be true that "He who is lost hesitates"? And how about "He snatched victory from the jaws of defeat"? Jokesters twist that around to become "He snatched defeat from the jaws of victory." In each case, the words are the same, but as the arrangement changes so does the meaning.

Word order is serious business. As an example, watch what happens when the word *only* is moved around as is done here:

- *Only* my car ran out of gas yesterday. (No other car in the world did.)
- My *only* car ran out of gas yesterday. (I have but one car.)
- My car ran out of gas *only* yesterday. (Some people will say this means "My car ran out of gas just yester-

day." Others will say it means "Yesterday was the one day my car ran out of gas," an idea that is made clearer in the next example.)

• My car ran out of gas yesterday *only*. (It happened but once.)

Word order can influence the meanings of words as well as the meanings of sentences. This is pointed out by Charlton Laird in *The Word.*[2] Laird uses these examples:

Fire the help.

Help the fire.

Of course, the sentences mean drastically different things, but look what happens to the words. In the first example, *fire* means "discharge"; in the second, *fire* means "conflagration." In the first example, *help* means "employees"; in the second, *help* means "assist."

When you have arranged words in the proper order, you have done your job right, and no one has a name for that. But where word order confuses meaning, the problem does have a name: *misplaced modifier.*

Misplaced:
And he remembered photographs of the hardened mud molds that had preserved the victims' final postures of terror and attempted flight for sixteen centuries. (Whatever these people were running from was so frightening that it gave birth to a new track and field event, the sixteen-hundred-year run.)
Better:
And he remembered photographs of the hardened mud molds that had preserved for sixteen centuries the victims' final postures of terror and attempted flight.

Misplaced:
He spent weeks away from home, often sleeping near a drilling rig in his car. (Crowded and messy.)
Better:
He spent weeks away from home, often sleeping in his car near a drilling rig.

Misplaced:
Staff members attended a March 26 meeting on formaldehyde that was organized by the governor's office. (Sounds like the governor organized formaldehyde.)
Better:
Staff members attended a meeting on problems associated with formaldehyde. The governor called the meeting, which was held on March 26.

Misplaced:
William Thomas, in his reply to Jim Morgan dated September 22, 1981, indicated that he was investigating the Division's activities. (Jim Morgan was not dated September 22.)
Better:
William Thomas, in his September 22, 1981, reply to Jim Morgan, indicated that he was investigating the Division's activities.

Misplaced:
Badges may be obtained by publishing personnel at the door. (You publish books or magazines. You do not publish personnel at the door, or anywhere.)
Better:
Publishing personnel may obtain badges at the door.

Misplaced:
Manufacturers of chemical mixtures with 250 em-

ployees or more have one year to evaluate and label mixtures. (Mixtures don't have employees.)
Better:
Chemical manufacturers who have 250 employees or more have one year to evaluate and label mixtures.

Misplaced:
No further action was taken until after the inspectors presented a report on the refinery's emissions at the December 20, 1982, Board meeting. (Sounds like the refinery emitted pollutants during a Board meeting.)
Better:
No further action was taken on the refinery's emissions until after the inspectors presented a report at the December 20, 1982, Board meeting.

Word order can also influence style, that elusive literary quality so sought after by writers. To many readers and writers, "a group of *good* children" is more forceful than "a *good* group of children." What this means is that we can juggle words to improve style. Sometimes the juggling can be done without altering meaning:

a new pair of shoes

a pair of new shoes

Both mean the same, but *"new* shoes" carries more force than "a *new* pair of shoes."

Similarly, elements in a series can be arranged for purposes of style. The first sample in the next pair builds to a climax by beginning with a one-syllable word, then going to a three-syllable word, then ending with a longer phrase. The expression can be written as in the second sample, but some intangible quality is lost.

- life, liberty, and the pursuit of happiness
- liberty, life, and the pursuit of happiness

Rearranging words can also be done to make a sentence read more easily. Note the difference in the flow of ideas in these examples:

- One purpose of the visit was to check on organization of the files *and content* (bad).
- One purpose of the visit was to check on organization *and content* of the files (better).

In short, word order can influence style, but the chief thought to keep in mind about word order is the one that was stated earlier: The arrangement of words in a sentence determines the meaning of that sentence.

Can problems of meaning ever be solved by a computer? Remember, the computer is competing with the human brain. Also remember that the English language consists of more than 500,000 words with an unknown number of meanings and an infinite number of ways of arranging these words. Then consider the results posted by an earlier computer that was fed this sentence:

Time flies like an arrow.

The computer responded by saying that the sentence had these meanings:

Time moves in the same manner that an arrow moves.
Measure the speed of flies in the same way that you measure the speed of an arrow.
Measure the speed of flies that resemble an arrow.

A particular variety of flies called "time-flies" are fond of an arrow.[3]

Computers have come a long way since that experiment was run two decades ago, but asking digital circuits to solve the complexities of meaning is a large order.

Be specific

3

Advice on what a fact is, writing about facts, abstract versus specific words, the unwise shifting of terms, avoiding Janus words, and the fine art of giving instructions. *Plus* a puzzle for you to solve and the reason why the Light Brigade rode to its doom.

It's important to be specific when we write, to tell people exactly what it is we want to tell them or exactly what it is they must do. Any degree of vagueness, no matter how small, can easily cause confusion and lead to a waste of time and money. For instance, the paragraph below is written in simple terms about an ordinary task—but can you guess what the task is?

The procedure is actually quite simple. First you arrange things into different groups. Of course, one pile may be sufficient depending on how much there is to do. If you have to go somewhere else due to lack of facilities, that is the next step, otherwise you are pretty well set. It is important not to overdo things. That is, it is better to do too few things at once than too many. In the short run this may not seem important but complications can easily arise. A mistake can be expensive as well. At first the whole procedure will seem complicated. Soon, however, it will become just another facet of life. It is difficult to foresee any end to the necessity for this task in the immediate future, but then one never can tell. After the procedure is completed, one arranges the materials into different groups again. Then they can be put into their appropriate places. Eventually they will be used once more and the whole cycle will then have to be repeated. However, that is part of life.[1]

If you said that the passage tells how to do the laundry, you're either remarkably perceptive or very lucky. What makes the passage hard to understand is the use of words with many meanings, words such as *procedure, things,* and *facilities.* Had the writer used *doing the laundry* instead of *procedure, dirty clothing* instead of *things,* and *washer and dryer* instead of *facilities*—the passage would have been something considerably better than a guessing game.

STATEMENTS OF FACT

A statement of fact is the cornerstone of being specific. Good writing is based on fact, and facts make up the foundation of any argument. As Jack Webb drawled repeatedly, in his role of Sergeant Joe Friday on the 1950s television series "Dragnet," "Just the facts, please, just the facts."

To work with facts, the writer must first identify them and then use the word *fact* correctly.

To identify a fact, we can begin by saying: A fact is an event or a statement of objective reality; a fact can be verified by observation or judged reasonably likely because of documentary evidence.

The street address of the house you live in is a fact.

This address is visible and real to any number of observers at any time. In addition, the address is recorded at the county seat and on any number of documents, such as the mortgage, the deed, insurance papers, and utility bills.

That the house is comfortable, spacious, airy, large, small, or just right—these are not statements of fact. These are opinions, and it is highly possible that no two observers would hold the same opinion.

An aid to identifying facts is to classify them as either *historical* or *scientific:*

Historical: the assassination of President Kennedy on November 22, 1963; the armistice terminating World War I on November 11, 1918; Napoleon's evacuation of Moscow in 1812. A historical fact can be verified by records written by observers then living.

Scientific: the temperature at which water freezes; the speed of light; the terminal velocity of a falling body in a vacuum. A scientific fact can be rechecked at any time and its validity established.

When writing, it might be best to omit the word *fact* and let the facts speak for themselves. When that cannot be done, the next best thing is to make certain that the word *fact* is not used to introduce sentences like these:

In fact, if Carter Oil could continue to dispose of its naphtha under satisfactory terms, the company's gasoline vending business would not be adversely affected.

As a matter of fact, a decrease in subcontracting might force Artprint out of business.

The fact is that General Technology will probably

experience instances of inability to market its products.

Those three statements are not statements of fact. Use of the words *could, would, might,* and *probably* make those statements into assumptions, opinions, or predictions.

Finally, don't be carried away with the importance of facts. Mark Twain did this once, as a gag, when he "proved" how the Mississippi River was going to move Cairo, Illinois, a thousand miles closer to New Orleans. But let him tell it in his own words:

> In the space of one hundred and seventy-six years the Lower Mississippi has shortened itself two hundred and forty-two miles. That is an average of a trifle over one mile and a third per year. Therefore, any calm person, who is not blind or idiotic, can see that in the Old Oölitic Silurian Period, just a million years ago next November, the Lower Mississippi River was upward of one million three hundred thousand miles long, and stuck out over the Gulf of Mexico like a fishing-rod. And by the same token any person can see that seven hundred and forty-two years from now the Lower Mississippi will be only a mile and three-quarters long, and Cairo and New Orleans will have joined their streets together, and be plodding comfortably along under a single mayor and a mutual board of aldermen. There is something fascinating about science. One gets such wholesale returns of conjecture out of such a trifling investment of fact.[2]

MAKING THE ABSTRACT INTO THE SPECIFIC

Many words are not factual or specific but instead *abstract.* An abstract word is one that has many meanings.

For instance, the word *church* can mean the church on the corner, the Roman Catholic church, or the whole tradition of institutionalized religion.

A word that has many meanings poses problems. The most obvious one of course is this: Which particular meaning do you want your readers to grasp? You also have to consider another problem that research has uncovered about abstract words; that is, abstract words are more difficult to remember than specific ones.[3]

The way to deal with these problems is to make the abstract into the specific. To do this, take the abstract word and define it by using specific words and terms.

For instance, the term *sloppy work* is a criticism that can cover many types of work and many degrees of sloppiness. Robert Pirsig, author of a best-selling book, *Zen and the Art of Motorcycle Maintenance,* was once the victim of some sloppy maintenance performed on his motorcycle. Instead of calling it sloppy work and leaving his readers wondering what he was writing about, Pirsig described the situation in these terms:

> The shop was a different scene from the ones I remembered. The mechanics, who had once all seemed like ancient veterans, now looked like children. A radio was going full blast and they were clowning around and talking and seemed not to notice me. When one of them finally came over he barely listened to the piston slap before saying, "Oh yeah. Tappets."
>
> Tappets? I should have known then what was coming.
>
> Two weeks later I paid their bill for 140 dollars, rode the cycle carefully at varying low speeds to wear it in and then after one thousand miles opened it up. At about seventy-five it seized again and freed

at thirty, the same as before. When I brought it back they accused me of not breaking it in properly, but after much argument agreed to look into it. They overhauled it again and this time took it out themselves for a high-speed road test.

It seized on *them* this time.

After the third overhaul two months later they replaced the cylinder, put in oversize main carburetor jets, retarded the timing to make it run as coolly as possible and told me, "Don't run it fast."

It was covered with grease and did not start. I found the plugs were disconnected, connected them and started it, and now there really *was* a tappet noise. They hadn't adjusted them. I pointed this out and the kid came with an open-end adjustable wrench, set wrong, and swiftly rounded both of the sheet-aluminum tappet covers, ruining both of them.

"I hope we've got some more of those in stock," he said.

I nodded.

He brought out a hammer and cold chisel and started to pound them loose. The chisel punched through the aluminum cover and I could see he was pounding the chisel right into the engine head. On the next blow he missed the chisel completely and struck the head with the hammer, breaking off a portion of two of the cooling fins.

"Just stop," I said politely, feeling this was a bad dream. "Just give me some new covers and I'll take it the way it is."

I got out of there as fast as possible, noisy tappets, shot tappet covers, greasy machine, down the road, and then felt a bad vibration at speeds over twenty. At the curb I discovered two of the four engine-mounting bolts were missing and a nut was missing from the third. The whole engine was hanging on by only one bolt. The overhead-cam chain-tensioner bolt was also missing, meaning it would have been hopeless to try to adjust the tappets anyway. Nightmare . . .

I found the cause of the seizures a few weeks later, waiting to happen again. It was a little twenty-five-cent pin in the internal oil-delivery system that had been sheared and was preventing oil from reaching the head at high speeds.[4]

Notice the specific descriptions—"covered with grease," "plugs were disconnected," "open-end adjustable wrench, set wrong," "pounding the chisel right into the engine head," "engine mounting bolts were missing," and so on. By the time you finish reading this passage, you have a very good idea of what sloppy work is.

A similar problem in being specific is that of describing, as an example, a person who is old. Each of us has a different idea of what *old* means and what an elderly person looks like. Here is Ernest Hemingway's description of one such person:

The old man was thin and gaunt with deep wrinkles in the back of his neck. The brown blotches of the benevolent skin cancer the sun brings from its reflection on the tropic sea were on his cheeks. The blotches ran well down the sides of his face and his hands had the deep-creased scars from handling heavy fish on the cords. But none of these scars were fresh. They were as old as erosions in a fishless desert.[5]

Again, the writing is specific, made so with expressions such as "deep wrinkles," "brown blotches of the benevolent skin cancer," and "deep-creased scars."

The practice of employing specific terms to explain abstract ideas is adaptable to on-the-job uses. Consider three terms business organizations are concerned with: *efficiency, morale,* and *safety.* These are abstract words. A worthwhile discussion of them requires that they be expressed in specific terms:

- *Efficiency.* Output, up or down, by how many units or what percentage, as compared to last year at this time, as compared to similar operations.
- *Morale.* Rates of absenteeism, sick leave usage, tardyism, turnover.
- *Safety.* The truck's brakes that do not work, the finger guard broken off of the paper cutter, the stuck latches on the fire exits.

Even money can be an abstract idea that needs to be made more specific. As an example, a writer for the *Chicago Tribune Magazine* decided that few people could understand an amount as large as a billion dollars. Therefore, the writer boiled the amount down to more common terms: "53 tons of $20 bills."[6]

THE UNWISE SHIFTING OF TERMS

Don't shift terms just for the sake of variety. All too often, the practice of shifting terms produces sentences like this:

> In twenty-nine *cases* test results were valid, while in three *instances* not enough data were obtained.

As a result of that sentence, readers are left to ponder the difference between a *case* and an *instance.* It would be better to write: "In twenty-nine cases test results were valid, while in three not enough data were obtained."

Another example:

In this region, summer temperatures normally linger until early November but at other times stay until late in the *penultimate* month.

Try writing *that* instead of *the penultimate,* and the message is conveyed more quickly and more clearly. Otherwise, the use of a word like *penultimate* brings out the best and the worst in readers. Some are smart enough to know that *penultimate* means "next to the last," and others will go to the trouble of looking the definition up. Others will go to no trouble at all and read on ahead, ignorant of what month the writer is referring to. Still others will get technical about the whole thing and complain that no month is truly next to last.

A more extreme example is the next one below. Its sentences are far too long for easy comprehension, and each sentence introduces a new term.

(1) Because few pressure relief valves leak, and because certain circumstances discussed earlier in this report are likely to cause leaks, the SCM has been designed to focus on chronically leaking pressure relief valves. (2) Pressure relief valves which have been identified as leaking and which have the equipment necessary to repair the relief valves without shutting down the process unit would be inspected quarterly and after venting, and repaired as necessary. (3) Those pressure relief valves which cannot be repaired on-line would be inspected during the two three-month periods prior to a scheduled process unit turnaround and after venting. (4) When a leak from a pressure relief valve in this category is discovered, the operator must take one of several actions to minimize the possibility of recurrence of the

leak or to allow repair of a leak while the process
unit is in operation.

Sentence (1) contains the term "chronically leaking
pressure relief valves." Sentence (2) is concerned with
"valves which have been identified as leaking." Sentence
(3) mentions valves "which cannot be repaired on-line."
These three classes of valves may be the same or they may
be different. Sentence (4) states "this category," a reference to the last category mentioned. Still, terms are
shifted so frequently that readers have the right to wonder if "this category" might not refer to any other valve
mentioned.

The practice of shifting terms allows readers to assume
that meanings are being shifted also. Therefore, a word
should be repeated if it is the right word and if repeating
it will avoid confusion. If the repetition sounds clumsy,
try a pronoun or recast the sentence.

Instead of	*Write*
Staff investigators cited the operator for his violation, and *staff investigators* warned the *operator* about repeated use.	Staff investigators cited the operator for his violation, and *they* warned *him* about repeated use.
The plaintiff alleged that she was deprived of her rights under the First *Amendment* and the Fourteenth *Amendment.*	The plaintiff alleged that she was deprived of her rights under the First and Fourteenth *Amendments.*
Variations occur at a higher *rate* or a lower *figure,* depending on circumstances.	Variations occur at a higher or lower *rate* depending on circumstances.

or

> Variations occur at a
> higher or lower *figure,*
> depending on
> circumstances.

AVOIDING JANUS WORDS

According to Roman mythology, Janus was a god of light
and sun. He opened the gates of heaven in the morning
and closed them in the evening. He was also the god of
doors and of the coming and going of traffic, a god who
could look in two directions at one time. The month of
January is named after Janus, for January looks back to
the year past and looks forward to the current year. In
art, Janus is depicted as two bearded faces placed back to
back and looking in opposite directions.

The English language has Janus words, words with
contrasting meanings. They should be used with care or
avoided altogether so as not to confuse readers. Some of
the more common Janus words are:

oversight. Oversight means "mistake" or "surveillance." Consider the sentence "As a result of its
oversight, the agency gets involved with rule-mak-
ing at the district level." Is the agency involved because of a mistake? This sentence can be made clear
by writing, "As a result of its *surveillance* role, the
agency . . ."

presently. Dictionaries show two meanings for
presently: "now" and "soon." The announcement
"We will *presently* hear from our guest speaker"
means either (1) "We will now hear from our guest
speaker" or (2) "We will soon hear from our guest
speaker."

Therefore, if you are writing about the present, use *now, currently,* or simply *is* or *are.* If your topic refers to the near future, use *soon* or *in a little while.*

sanction. Sanction refers to "approval" or "penalty." Two meanings are attached to this sentence: "His conduct is *sanctioned* by the law." If his conduct is approved, say so. If it's penalized, say so. Don't let readers figure things out for themselves.

since. Since refers to time: "Since the end of World War II, military strength in this country has steadily declined." *Since* also refers to cause and is a synonym for *because.* A good practice is to use *because* in causal situations, for just the sight of the word plants the notion of cause rather than time in the reader's mind.

Justification for this practice can be found in sentences like: *"Since* the law was changed, the number of arrests for drunk driving has increased 10.2 percent." Does this mean *"Since* the *date* the law was changed . . ."* or *"Because* the law was changed . . ."*?

verbal. A *verbal* message can be spoken or written. A letter that contains the statement "We have *verbally* agreed to start Program X on May 10" allows the reader two choices: (1) We spoke about Program X, but May 10 isn't written down, so it's not binding; or (2) We agreed in writing, and therefore May 10 is binding. Confusion can be avoided by using statements such as: "as we agreed over the telephone"; "according to our conversation of April 4"; or "as you wrote in your letter of April 4."

while. While has a meaning that refers to two events going on at the same time, as in, *"While* the others worked, he went fishing." *While* is also used in place of *although* to stand for "though" or "in spite of the fact that." This second usage of *while* weakens writing and allows different interpretations of sentences such as these: *"While* laws have mandated agencies to provide reasonable accommodation, no guidance has been written" and *"While* this authority is limited, the influence on the decision may be substantial." If *although* is meant, that's the word that should be used.

THE FINE ART OF GIVING INSTRUCTIONS

When giving instructions, use *shall* or *must* for actions that are imperative. Use *should* for actions that are optional but recommended. Use *may* to say that something is permitted. As examples:

Employees *must* limit their breaks to two per day. (The break policy is firm. Don't take any more than two each day.)

Employees *should* limit their breaks to two per day. (The break policy is flexible, but we don't want you away from your desks too often.)

Employees *may* take more than two breaks per day. (It's up to you how many breaks you take.)

When giving instructions, make every word specific, not only the *shalls* and *musts.* Even the word *the,* a specific word meaning "that thing I'm pointing to or talking about," is at times not specific enough. This we learn from the example set by Lord Raglan.

Raglan commanded British troops at Balaclava during the Crimean War of 1854. A short battle left him with a problem. Russian cavalry had captured some of his artillery, and Raglan wanted the guns back. No general likes to lose artillery, especially when he's a British general being watched by French allies to see what he'll do next.

A small force would do the trick. Such a force happened to be handy—a light cavalry brigade of 673 brightly uniformed, saber-bearing, professional soldiers, the kind who cheered when ordered to "Fight or die where you stand," the kind who had been frustrated by weeks of inactivity while their comrades garnered glory and medals.

So Raglan dictated a written order and sent it into the valley where his cavalry brigade waited. The order, scribbled in haste on a light blue leaf torn from a notebook, read:

> Lord Raglan wishes the cavalry to advance rapidly to the front, and try to prevent the enemy carrying away the guns. Troop of Horse Artillery may accompany. French cavalry is on your left. Immediate.[7]

The order raises these questions. Was the Horse Artillery to accompany, or wasn't it? The sentence "Troop of Horse Artillery may accompany" is nowhere near as definite as saying ". . . the Horse Artillery must accompany" or ". . . the Horse Artillery shall accompany." And "French cavalry is on your left" can mean that the "French cavalry will ride your left" or that the "French cavalry is standing fast on your left." As for the opening "Lord Raglan wishes," use of the word *wishes* is polite and weak but acceptable, for in military service, a wish is a command.

But the major fault is this: "prevent the enemy carrying away the guns." *Which* guns? The guns Raglan wanted back were in four lightly defended redoubts on the slopes to one side of the valley. There were other guns, however, heavily defended Russian guns at the far end of the valley. Raglan didn't specify which guns; he simply said *the* guns.

Lord Cardigan, commander of the Light Brigade, misunderstood the order and led his men past the captured artillery and into the point-blank fire of 3,000 Russians. The fight lasted twenty minutes. It ended when the British retreated, forty percent of their men dead or wounded or captured, and almost all of the brigade's horses killed or having to be destroyed.[8]

And as words failed then, so do words keep alive the memory of that event, in the poem "The Charge of the Light Brigade," by Alfred, Lord Tennyson:

> *Into the Valley of Death*
> *Rode the six hundred. . . .*
> *Theirs not to reason why,*
> *Theirs but to do and die.[9]*

Make relationships clear

4

Advice on rewriting illogical
statements into logical ones,
spreading out noun strings,
avoiding the telegraphic style,
putting *that* into your writing,
filling various verbal gaps, and
matching nouns and pronouns.
Plus "logic" as defined by *The
Devil's Dictionary*; also, the
boiled baby syndrome.

In *The Devil's Dictionary,* Ambrose Bierce defined logic as "the art of thinking and reasoning in strict accordance with the limitations and incapacities of the human misunderstanding. The basis of logic is the syllogism, consisting of a major and a minor premise and a conclusion—thus:

> "*Major Premise:* Sixty men can do a piece of work sixty times as quickly as one man.
> "*Minor Premise:* One man can dig a post-hole in sixty seconds; therefore—
> "*Conclusion:* Sixty men can dig a post-hole in one second." [1]

FROM ILLOGICAL TO LOGICAL

Bierce's piece of illogicality is intentional, of course, meant to be a joke. Most other illogical statements are unintentional, the faulty products of hasty thinking and writing. Straight thinking prevents such illogical statements; rewriting clears them up once they're on paper. As examples:

Because nearly all fifty-eight counties have cropland within their boundaries, only the major agricultural areas were selected for study. (Why were the major areas selected for study? Not because nearly all counties have cropland. Instead: "The major agricultural areas were selected for study because they would yield the most information.")

Since most of my experience has been in the federal government, I would welcome an opportunity to work in state government. (This sentence literally says, "I've worked for the feds for a while; now I want to try the state." The writer has not shown the relationship. The sentence would make more sense and stand a better chance of getting the writer a job if it read: "My experience in the federal government is an asset I can bring to state government.")

Having raised a family of six children, the company's treasurer and his wife live in the Glen Greens area. (Having raised a family of six children, the company treasurer and his wife could live elsewhere too. The two ideas in this sample are unrelated. They need to be separated and placed in their proper places in the same document.)

Because we have 48,000 members and because we offer so many services, it is often difficult to get the word out. (It could be difficult to get the word out for a variety of reasons. There may be no one who has time to write up the word, there may be no funds for mailing, or the printing press may be broken. But to blame this failure on the number of services is bad management. And to blame the failure on the 48,000 members is bad public relations.)

New members will be introduced, and hors d'oeuvres will be served. (Grammar teachers call this faulty coordination; that is, the parts of the sentence should not be joined by the word *and*. Regardless of what the error is called, if you were a new member, how would you like to be ranked with the hors d'oeuvres?)

NOUN STRINGS

In the name of brevity, writers occasionally omit the little words that show relationships. An example is the noun string:

> Colorado School of Mines Potential Gas Agency estimates ... (this should be rewritten as: "Estimates *made by the* Potential Gas Agency *of the* Colorado School of Mines ..." or "Estimates *made by the* Colorado School of Mines' Potential Gas Agency ...")

By rewriting to include the italicized words, both the second and third versions are easier to read than the original.

Writers of noun strings should heed the rebuke issued years ago by John R. Baker, a faculty member of the Department of Zoology at Oxford. Baker said of the noun string: "These are words put together without the slightest attempt at clarity or consideration for the reader. The phrase is worse than merely illiterate: it is rude." [2]

In fact, the noun string is worse than illiterate or rude;

it has been proven to be hard to understand.[3] Therefore, noun strings should be spread out and the reader given clues as to what the meaning is:

Noun string	*Spread out*
Sampled wine fermenting batch	Batch of fermenting wine that was sampled
Uncontrolled particle size data	Data on uncontrolled particle size
Ground water data activities (This has two meanings; see right column.)	Data on ground water activities *or* Activities necessary to gather data on ground water

And then there is this monster:

The Okanogan Timber Supply Area Yield Report Summary

which would be far easier to read if rearranged in this manner:

Summary of a Report on the Yield of the Okanogan Timber Supply Area

TELEGRAPHIC STYLE

A similar problem occurs when writers use the *telegraphic style*. The telegraphic style is useful to save space or to impart vigor to newspaper headlines. Otherwise, it is a style that makes for rough reading:

Telegraphic	*Spread out*
Lighting was such that field team decided to terminate activities.	Lighting was such that *the* field team decided to terminate *its* activities.
Use puller to remove bearing.	Use *a* puller to remove *the* bearing.
Plans made by staff include . . .	Plans made by *the* staff include . . .

ABSENT *THAT*

Another gap that needs to be filled in is the absent *that*. There's a school of thought that says, "Leave out the word *that* whenever possible." The idea is to produce a sentence that is shorter and simpler to read. When this theory is followed, "He knew that he could do it" becomes "He knew he could do it."

What the research shows is something different, for sentences where *that* is retained are easier to understand than those sentences where *that* is dropped.[4] As an example, "He said *that* things were going well" is easier to understand than "He said things were going well."

It's a small point, perhaps, but one that could have a lot to do with clarity.

AN ASSORTMENT OF ABSENCES

Try to picture this in your mind: "We will mix the brass and copper cleaner in a 5-gallon pail until we have filled a 55-gallon drum." Tricky, isn't it? You'll have to use your imagination to move the cleaner from the pail to the drum.

The writer has omitted a few words, which is all too

easy to do. Unfortunately, the gaps lead to rough reading at the least and misunderstanding at the worst. A few other gaps that need filling in are:

Messy agenda. "Senator Adlai Stevenson, chairman of the space and science subcommittee, has announced that he will introduce legislation in January, ensuring that yet a third session of Congress will have genes on its agenda." (For a quick fix, try: "the *subject of* genes.")

Fruit basket. "Low-solvent gravure inks are now used successfully. In many cases, printing press speeds equal to solvent inks have been achieved." (Mixing press speeds and solvent inks in the second sentence is like mixing apples and oranges. The second sentence should read, ". . . press speeds equal to *those obtainable with* solvent inks have been achieved.")

Impatient petrochemicals. "Petrochemicals can't wait! . . . Petrochemicals can't wait anymore." (Petrochemicals aren't that impatient; the people who run the petrochemical industry are: "The petrochemical *industry* can't wait!")

Sneaky meter. "Watch water meter for movement." (It's not the meter that moves, it's the pointer. Write, "Watch the water meter's *pointer* for movement.")

Even buildings get nervous. Title of a bulletin: "To All Employees at Alarmed Facilities." (Facilities don't become alarmed; people do. What is meant here is: "To All Employees at Facilities with Alarms.")

New way to save paperwork. "A fireplace and stove monitoring program is unlikely to result in burning restrictions, officials said today." (To make this sentence better, write, "restrictions on burning.")

And the worst of all possible gaps is this one: "By methods too complicated to discuss here, we estimated the probability and consequences of these [events, occurrences, accidents, ???]." Translation: "Take my word for it, folks."

MATCHING NOUNS AND PRONOUNS

Careful usage requires writers to make a pronoun refer to its *antecedent*. An antecedent is the noun or noun phrase that comes immediately before the pronoun. This relationship can be seen in sentence 1:

1. The staff submitted its recommendation to *the district,* but *it* took no action for six months.

In sentence 1, *the district* is the antecedent noun phrase, and the word *it* is the pronoun. The sentence says that the district took no action for six months.

But is that what the writer meant? The first thought in the sentence is an active, substantial one that carries weight throughout the sentence: "The staff submitted its recommendation." The second thought is a passive one: "took no action." Also, the pronoun *it* is one of the weakest of words. Accordingly, readers have the right to stop at *it* and suspect that the writer was careless with applying the rule of pronoun reference and really meant that the staff took no action.

If district is meant, the sentence can be made clearer and stronger by repeating the word *district:*

2. The staff submitted its recommendation to the

district, but the district took no action for six
months.

If staff is meant, drop the pronoun *it:*

    3. The staff submitted its recommendation to the
district but took no action for six months.

Not recommended is the awkward use of parenthetical
repetition in an attempt to ensure understanding:

    4. The staff submitted its recommendation to the
district, but it (the staff) took no action for six
months.

Also not recommended in this instance is the use of the
word *which:*

    5. The staff submitted its recommendation to the
district, *which* took no action for six months.

The use of *which* in sentence 5 allows readers to make two
interpretations: (1) The staff submitted its recommendation before a particular district took no action or (2) a
particular district did nothing after the staff submitted
its recommendation.

    The careless use of *this* (or *that*) can lead to confusion:

    6. The safe driving campaign had little influence,
cost a great deal of money, and used up large
amounts of time. *This* leads to pessimism about any
further campaigns. (Does *this* refer to the lack of influence, the cost, the time used up, or all three?
What was probably meant was: *"These three* effects
lead to pessimism about any further campaigns.")

The best practice to follow is to use pronouns only
when necessary, place them as close to their antecedents

as possible, and take pains to make certain that relationships are clear. Otherwise, a writer's efforts may produce
sentences such as:

7. If the baby does not thrive on fresh milk it
should be boiled.[5]

Be positive

5

Advice on writing positive statements, a variety of negative forms, getting rid of cringing, getting rid of *al* and *ly*, and ending discrimination against language. Plus a school-days' joke about the double negative.

Remember teacher saying, "Don't use double negatives"? And as soon as we were out of the classroom we changed teacher's admonition to, "Don't use *no* double negatives."

FROM NEGATIVE TO POSITIVE

Of course, teacher was right. In fact, teacher was more right than is generally known, for readability research has shown that comprehension is reduced when writers use negative expressions such as:

1. The double negative. "We are *not un*aware of the expertise and dedication that Ms. Alexander brings to her position."
2. The single obvious negative. "Black is *not* a light color."
3. The single hidden negative. "There are *few* (*not* many) hours left."
4. The single negative qualifier. "They would have walked home *except* for the rain." [1]

Examples 1 and 2 can easily be rewritten in positive form to improve comprehension.

Negative:
1. We are *not un*aware of the expertise and dedication that Ms. Alexander brings to her position.
Positive:
1. We are aware of the expertise and dedication that Ms. Alexander brings to her position.

Negative:
2. Black is *not* a light color.
Positive:
2. Black is a dark color.

Can examples 3 and 4 be rewritten in positive form? Possibly, but it would take completely different wording at the risk of drastically altering meanings.

The effort to eliminate negative expressions becomes even more important when a sentence contains a triple negative. Rewriting the negative samples below makes them shorter and easier to understand.

Negative:
The expansion of this program would *never* have been accomplished *unless* the district manager and his staff had *not* carefully planned for it.
Positive:
The expansion of this program was accomplished only because the district manager and his staff carefully planned for it.

Negative:
Unless an employee uses more than two consecutive days of sick leave, *except* where an employee has a demon-

strated pattern of sick leave abuse, he or she shall *not* be required to provide a doctor's verification.

Positive:

When an employee with a demonstrated pattern of sick leave abuse uses more than two consecutive days of sick leave, he or she shall be required to provide a doctor's verification.

Another form of negative expression is the *negative of measurement*. Those can usually be rewritten in positive form.

Negative:
no less than five
Positive:
at least five
five or more
a minimum of five

Negative:
no more than five
Positive:
a maximum of five
five at the most

Care must be taken when rewriting a negative statement into positive form so as not to change the statement's meaning. An example is a sentence like "I am *not* looking for work." This can mean (1) "I have a job," or (2) "I don't have a job and I don't want one." It would be wrong to rewrite "I am *not* looking for work" into positive form without knowing the facts.

In addition to teacher saying, "Don't use double negatives," teacher also said, "Don't change anything unless you're sure of the meaning."

GETTING RID OF CRINGING

Cringing is another way to be negative. To be certain, some degree of caution is required. For instance, it is usually wrong to be so bold as to write *all, none, true, false, never, always,* or any similar absolute expression. Rarely can a statement containing one of those words stand close inspection. The writer of the line "there being *no* way to prove such assumptions" would be better off writing "there being *no* way known to this author to prove such assumptions." And the midwesterner who declares, "It *never* snows around these parts before Thanksgiving," is easily proved wrong in the fall when a blizzard strikes well before turkey day.

On the other hand, unnecessary caution only serves to weaken the writer's style and the argument embodied in that style. When this happens, the writer has cringed. Cringing can be corrected, usually quite easily:

Oil enters the tank somewhat continuously. (Continuous is continuous; there's no "somewhat" about it. What the writer probably means is, "The flow of oil into the tank is seldom interrupted.")

Two staff members collected three samples each—upwind, downwind, and intermediate. (*Crosswind* is the logical word in place of "intermediate." Readers are used to *crosswind,* but "intermediate" wind?)

It can be expected that sludge may burn less evenly than coal. (The author is being too tentative. Strike out "It can be expected," and say, "Sludge may burn less evenly than coal.")

Possible sun caused disparity between factors for 2P and 2S. (The sun is not only "possible," it is; it exists. What is meant is, "The presence [or absence] of sunshine may have caused disparity between 2P and 2S.")

It seems that it might possibly be wise to establish a new procedure. (Write, "It might be wise to establish a new procedure.")

A mild form of cringing is the scholarly type that goes "I would like to point out," "I would like to acknowledge," "I would like to thank," or "I would like to recommend." The word *would* makes these statements conditional, and the readers of such statements have every right to demand, "Well, darn it, you ought to say, 'I will point out,' 'I acknowledge,' 'I thank,' or 'I recommend.' "

Finally, there is this ultimate cringe, which is pure bureaucratic nonspeak:

The practice does not appear to be widespread. On the other hand, it does not appear to be isolated either.

From reading these two sentences, we know nothing about "the practice," but we do know a lot about the writer. Here is a person who is talking about nonappearances, thereby leaving us to wonder if "the practice" exists. Here is a person who cannot admit, at least in these two sentences, "I don't know."

GETTING RID OF *AL* AND *LY*

Words ending in *al* or *ly* weaken writing by allowing readers to make the criticisms shown in parentheses.

al

Most victims die from smoke inhalation before the *actual* fire ever reaches them. (Drop *actual*. A fictitious fire doesn't kill.)

The engineer then compared *actual* volume of gas collected to what was expected. (Change *actual* to *measured* and write, "The engineer then compared *measured* volume of gas to what was expected.")

The system is in *actual* line operation. (The operation is *actual* without need for an extra word.)

Personnel reports often contain statements such as "has an *exceptional* understanding of all phases of the job" or "*exceptional* skill in directing others." (The problem is, is the person exceptionally good or exceptionally bad?)

Mutual agreement. (That's the only kind there is.)

Functional organizational charts. (Are there dysfunctional organizational charts?)

Residential house. (Redundant. Just call it a house.)

Intellectual knowledge. (Again, the only kind there is.)

Terminological notes. (Simply, notes on terms.)

ly

Refrigeration has been *effectively* used to remove gaseous pollutants. (Would the pollutants be removed if refrigeration had been used ineffectively?)

Specifically designed for this use. (A design is specific. There's no need to elaborate on it.)

I am *thoroughly* familiar with the printing process. (There is no such thing as being "thoroughly familiar." The choice is either *familiar* or *know*.)

Relatively low doses are *typically* encountered at the ambient level. (How relative and how typical?)

Statistically recalculating a use factor. (Does this mean to recalculate the statistics or to use statistical methods when recalculating?)

Almost *exactly* identical. (Wordy. Say, "Almost identical.")

When the meat is cooked to your pleasure [when making stew], you may wish to add a cup of *thoroughly* mixed water. (Why not write, "Thoroughly mix in a cup of water"?)

On February 23, 1982, the staff visited three highway bridges that *recently* had been repainted. (*Recently* in this report meant 1979, three years earlier.)

ENDING DISCRIMINATION AGAINST LANGUAGE

It is appropriate to alter masculine titles that apply to jobs held by men or women. We have become used to *supervisor* for *foreman, letter carrier* for *mailman, sales representative* for *salesman,* and other usages, as strange as they may have seemed at first.

On the other hand, there is a lot wrong with *he/she, s/he, her/his,* and *he or she.* They introduce waffling into the language and take the zip out of it. None of them is as easy to read as a single pronoun, and page after page of them proves tiring to readers. Further, the first three are difficult if not ridiculous to pronounce: Who wants to say "he slant she"?

No reason exists to write in this manner other than laziness or lack of linguistic conscience. Writers in educational and governmental organizations seem to be the worst offenders, perhaps because the law tells them not to discriminate in matters of gender, while no law requires them to be discriminating when it comes to language.

Regardless of where found or why, this wrongful discrimination against language can be made right by relatively simple means:

ELIMINATE PRONOUNS ALTOGETHER

Instead of	*Write*
An employee must use *his or her* compensatory time off within twelve months of it being earned.	An employee must use compensatory time off within twelve months of it being earned. (An employee cannot use someone else's time off.)
The licensing officer shall exercise *his* authority to issue permits by . . .	The licensing officer shall exercise *the* authority to issue permits by . . .

USE A SYNONYM

He/she works smoothly and efficiently without disrupting the routine.	The *employee* works smoothly and efficiently without disrupting the routine.

RECAST INTO THE PLURAL

Give each trainee *his* paper as soon as *he* is finished.	Give trainees *their* papers as soon as *they* are finished.

USE THE SECOND PERSON (*YOU* OR *YOUR*)

Anyone who wants to go to the office party should bring *his* money tomorrow.	If *you* want to go to the office party, *you* should bring *your* money tomorrow.

Do not, however, violate a fundamental principle of grammar by mixing singular with plural.

Incorrect	*Correct*
Require an *employee* (singular) to pick up *their* (plural) paychecks. (Instead of *"his* paycheck.")	Require *employees* (plural) to pick up *their* (plural) paychecks.

All in all, it is not hard to end wrongful discrimination against language, and to write firm, positive prose.

VERBS! VERBS! VERBS!

6

Advice on strong verbs versus
weak verbs, verbs that become
nouns, active versus passive
voice, agreement of subject and
verb, and the need to rely on
good, old-fashioned *verbs, verbs,
verbs.* Plus R. Buckminster Fuller
on "God is a verb."

R. Buckminster Fuller was an architect and engineer
best known for his development of the geodesic dome.
Fuller also wrote poetry, and one of his poems is "No
More Secondhand God," which contains these lines:

> *Yes, God is a verb,*
> *the most active,*
> *connoting the vast harmonic*
> *reordering of the universe*
> *from unleashed chaos of energy.*[1]

It's an intriguing thought, isn't it? According to all
that we've been taught in school, the word *God* signifies a
noun—a person, place, or thing. But Fuller says "God is
a verb," a force, an active agent, a doer of things.

Suppose we try to turn Fuller's words around and say,
"A verb is God." That doesn't work. When we write *"a
verb,"* we mean only one verb. Which verb? To make the
statement refer to all verbs, we would have to write,

"Verbs are gods." And that sounds pompous, simplistic, and perhaps heretical.

Still, if writers were to enshrine one part of speech, that part of speech should be the verb. It is the verb that imparts action and vigor to writing. It is the verb that gives force to writing. It is the verb that keeps the writing moving. It is the verb that carries readers along.

STRONG VERBS, NOT WEAK ONES

But, you say, business writing is basically dull. A memo is not high-powered suspense fiction, and a report is not a fast-paced western. When the topics are so ordinary, certainly, verbs can't be all that important.

Wrong! Wrong! Wrong!

Consider the difference between strong verbs and weak ones. A strong verb is one that hits its mark. A weak verb is one that has so many meanings that it waters down writing.

An example of a weak verb is *indicate. Indicate* can mean:

allude to	designate
argue	detail
attest	direct attention to
beckon	earmark
bespeak	express
betoken	hint
bring forward	imply
connote	intimate
convey	itemize
declare	label
demonstrate	make known
denote	manifest

mark
meant
note
particularize
point at
point out
point to
point forward
presage
prove
purport
reveal
say
show
signal

signify
speak of
speak to
specify
stand for
state
suggest
symbolize
tell
testify
touch on
typify
underscore
warn

More than one meaning can be attached to the statement, "Board members *indicated* that they would consider the matter at a later meeting." Think how much more accurate and forceful that statement would be if it read:

Board members *declared* ... (Strong. They definitely said so.)

Board members *made it known* ... (Strong. They publicized the event.)

Board members *said* (*stated*) ... (A little weaker. *Said* and *stated* are definite, but do not carry the same force as does *declared*.)

Board members *hinted* (*implied*) ... (Weakest, but depending upon the situation, could be the most honest.)

A similar argument can be made over the verb *increase*. Some writers, especially those who wish to be cau-

tious, overwork *increase*. Variety and clarity are better
served by writing:

accumulate	expand
add	extend
add to	fatten
advance	fill out
aggrandize	gain
aggravate	gain height
amplify	gain in circumference
ascend	gain in diameter
augment	gain in numbers
become better	gain strength
become bigger	gain weight
become larger	germinate
become wider	grow
become worse	grow bigger
bloat	grow larger
blow up	grow longer
boost	grow out
burgeon	grow up
deepen	inflate
deploy	intensify
develop	lengthen
dilate	lift
disperse	magnify
distend	multiply
double	outgrow
elevate	overrun
enhance	pad
enlarge	promote
enrich	puff up
exacerbate	pump up
exaggerate	raise
exalt	redouble

spread	thicken
strengthen	triple
stretch	widen
swell	

And then there is *involved in,* another popular phrase. Readers seeing *involved in* are not exactly sure of what is going on: "The Southern California Gas Company is *involved in* a NOx reduction test program for stationary internal combustion engines." Does this mean that the company is participating in the program, conducting the program, or merely thinking about it? The better writer would use the most accurate verb.

Another weak verb form is the *submerged verb.* A submerged verb is a verb that has been turned into a noun. When that happens, out goes the action imparted by the verb, and the passage becomes limp and wordy. In the samples below, the nouns are italicized and shown in the left column. The column on the right shows the nouns brought to the surface as verbs.

Submerged	*Surfaced*
by the *maintenance* of records	by *maintaining* records
difficulties in the *administration* of	difficulties in *administering*
a *resumption* of operations will	*resuming* operations will
a *reduction* of operating costs can	*reducing* operating costs can
the *design* of technical presentations and literature	*designing* technical presentations and literature

Still another verb form that weakens writing is the form made up of *it is, there is, there are,* and so on. These constructions can frequently be made stronger.

Weak	Stronger
It is our understanding that the project is on time.	We understand that the project is on time.
There is no need for a detailed investigation.	A detailed investigation is not necessary.
There are no changes to be made.	No changes are to be made.

Using an *it is, there is, there are,* or similar construction is not always wrong. Consider this sentence: "It is difficult to know when the budget will be approved." How else could you write it? "We don't know when ..."? The word *we* is too limiting; the *it is* phrase stands for a larger group of people than *we.* How about, "When the budget will be approved is not known"? That version sounds stiffer than the original and hides until the end a key point: the lack of knowledge. In this case, the writer's purpose could be better served by writing *it is.*

ACTIVE VERSUS PASSIVE VOICE

Voice is a term used to show how a sentence is arranged around its verb or verb phrase. Voice can be *active* or *passive.*

In active voice, the underlying logic is who did what to whom. In active voice, the emphasis is on the doer of the action, the agent, the acting force. When passive voice is used, the who-does-what order is reversed, and the focus of the sentence is changed to emphasize the object of the action. In the examples below, the DOER OF THE ACTION IS CAPITALIZED, *the verb or verb phrase is italicized,* and the object of the action is lowercased.

Active	*Passive*
THE OPERATOR *turned off* the computer.	The computer *was turned off* by THE OPERATOR.
THE DIVISION CHIEF *reprimanded* the staff.	The staff *was reprimanded* by THE DIVISION CHIEF.
TWO MEN *are painting* the storeroom.	The storeroom *is being painted* by TWO MEN.

Notice what happens. When an active-voice sentence is rewritten in passive form, it picks up words, becomes longer. Notice also that the passive form runs contrary to much of the way we think. That is, we live in an active-voice world. WE *drive* cars. WE *run* for exercise. GUNMEN *rob* banks. As children, the first sentences we learned to read were written in active voice: "TOM AND JANE *went* to the store."

In other words, a lot can be said for active voice and against passive voice. And a lot has. As editors and teachers endlessly proclaim, active voice brings life to writing and makes prose move along. Passive voice is wordy and tiring to read and a sure cure for insomnia. Worse, far too much business and scientific writing is in the passive voice, and it is the passive voice that makes documents deadly dull to read.

The claimed advantages for active voice as well as the justification for complaints against passive voice are both supported by research that dates back to the early 1960s. A large body of this research shows that in many instances active-voice sentences are easier to understand and remember than passive-voice sentences. Some additional research shows that passive sentences are easier to understand and remember when the intent is to focus on the object of the action, not the acting force.[2] Moreover, the ratio of active to passive verbs in "professional modern prose" has been estimated to be about three active verbs to every passive one.[3]

Therefore, it is not possible to universally condemn passive voice, as some critics do. And it is not practical to write every sentence in active voice. What is needed instead is the purposeful variety that can be obtained by mixing active and passive voices. As examples, here are two paragraphs from an issue of *The Wall Street Journal,* a well-written and well-edited paper. The italicized sentences are those in active voice.

Underscoring the problems the president faces in Congress, a House Appropriations subcommittee yesterday cut $30 million from the administration's request to funnel $60 million in military aid to El Salvador from funds earmarked for other countries. A separate request for $50 million in new aid for El Salvador earlier was cut out entirely by the House Foreign Affairs Committee.

The validity of some of the commission's criticism was questioned by the National Association of Secondary School Principals, which noted that more students are taking additional English, math and science classes today than is reflected in the data on which the commission relied. *However, Scott Thomson, executive director of the organization, welcomed the unfavorable comparison of U.S. schools with schools in other industrialized nations, saying it would help dispel the popular belief "that we're the best."*[4]

In short, a lot depends upon what you want to emphasize—agent or object. Suppose your dog bit the President of the United States. You might say, "My dog bit the President"—a sentence purely in active voice. But a newspaper reporter would know that to millions of Americans the President is more important than your dog. Therefore, the reporter's sentence would read, "The President was bitten by a dog"—straight passive voice.

Where passive voice has picked up a bad name is when the agent drops out of the picture. You see this kind of writing in sentences that begin: "It has been decided . . ." or "A decision has been reached . . ." Those sentences don't make sense, for we know that someone, some person or organization, decided or reached a decision. Decisions don't just materialize out of thin air.

Therefore, it would be far better to write, "We have reached a decision" or "The committee has decided." That same principle holds true for sentences like these next two examples. Without an agent, they simply don't sound sensible.

Passive	*Active*
The efficiency was calculated by the ratio of sampled concentrations to ambient concentrations. (The ratio did not do the calculating.)	To calculate the efficiency, *we* used the ratio of sampled concentrations to ambient concentrations.
February was spent visiting retail paint	During February *we* (staff members) visited

outlets such as Lumberjack, Sears, and Standard Brands. (February was not spent, expended, or used; someone did something during February.)	retail paint outlets such as . . .

Sometimes, however, an agent is not necessary. When you're looking for the photocopy machine, it is important to know that "The machine is located down the hallway," a passive-voice sentence. In this case, who put the machine there is not important. Similarly, "The office was redecorated last year"; who did the work is not important, unless you have a complaint or compliment concerning the decorator.

If you feel bounced around by the question of whether to use active or passive voice, just remember this: Active voice makes for strong, vigorous writing. Write most of your sentences in the active voice, and don't use the passive voice unless you have an excellent reason for doing so.

AGREEMENT OF SUBJECT AND VERB

A subject and its verb must agree in number. That is, a singular subject takes a singular verb, and a plural subject takes a plural verb. Two of the simplest examples are:

Singular: *This* program *is* out of date.
Plural: *These* programs *are* out of date.

Words that intervene between the subject and the verb do not affect the number of the verb:

Wrong	*Right*
Property acquired through donations and transfers, including 350 acres of land and several buildings, *are* not described in this report.	*Property* acquired through donations and transfers, including 350 acres of land and several buildings, *is* not described in this report.
The record of changes and valuations *are* kept . . .	*The record* of changes and valuations *is* kept . . .

The word *none* sometimes causes problems in agreement. These problems can be avoided by thinking of *none* as meaning "not one":

Wrong	*Right*
None of the engines *are* acceptable.	*None* (not one) of the engines *is* acceptable.

Another problem arises with a compound subject, one formed of two or more nouns joined by *and*. In almost all cases, a compound subject is thought of as a plural:

Wrong	*Right*
The duct and the stack is tested daily.	*The duct and the stack are* tested daily.

However, using *or* in place of *and* does not make a subject compound, and this sentence is correct: "The duct *or* the stack *is* tested daily."

As is usual with the English language, rules don't work in all situations, and peculiarities of usage take over. As examples, both of the following are correct:

The *contents* of the room *is* one chair.
The contents of the room *are* several pieces of furniture.

Both of those sentences will sound better, however, and also avoid problems with agreement, if written:

The room contains one chair.
The room contains several pieces of furniture.

These last examples demonstrate what this chapter is about. Admittedly, *contains* is not the world's greatest verb. Still, by using *contains,* the sentences under question have become shorter, more to the point, stronger, easier to read, and pose no problems of agreement. Overall, a lot of problems in writing can be solved by relying on good, old-fashioned *verbs, verbs, verbs.*

Keep shoptalk in the shop

7

Advice on the need to keep shoptalk in the shop, jargon that can be written in plain English, how the confusion factor increases when jargon means different things in different professions, and translations from the legalese. *Plus* jargon and the Texas Utilities Company, a legal opinion written in plain English, and comments on legalese by Will Rogers, Abraham Lincoln, Thomas Jefferson, and Jonathan Swift.

There's a story about shoptalk that begins with an incident that happened at a boiler operated by the Texas Utilities Company. The boiler, about the size of a thirty-story office building, used enormous quantities of oxygen to support combustion. To provide the oxygen, large fans pushed air into the boiler, and other large fans pulled air out. The fans pushing air into the boiler stopped working one day. The fans pulling air out continued to work and caused a vacuum that sucked the walls in about four feet.

Trent C. Root, Jr., vice president of the company, said, "Since this particular unit has a low fuel cost and it materially affects the billing to our customers, we felt they deserved to know what happened. So we asked the engineers in our generating company to write a news release. Let me quote that release to you.

NEGATIVE FURNACE EXCURSION

UNIT #1 MLSES

JULY 21, 1977

At 0216 hours July 21, 1977, a negative furnace excursion occurred on Unit #1. This occurred when two of the I.D. fans tripped while the unit was at full load.

This boiler automatically goes into a unit runback condition when this occurs.

The closing of dampers plus the reduction of the furnace fires created a vacuum condition in the boiler which resulted in some tube leaks and slight structural damage.

There were no malfunctions during this incident. These controls responded as they were designed to do.

The unit will be out of service between three to four weeks.

"So you can see we are still learning to communicate," Root said, continuing with, "Needless to say, this news release was completely rewritten." [1]

The news release was rewritten because it said nothing about changes in customers' bills. That was its principal fault. But look at the shoptalk: "negative furnace excursion"; "I.D. fans" (an unexplained abbreviation); "tripped"; "unit run-back." These terms would have meant nothing to the customer, even if the billing had been explained.

The moral of the story is: Keep shoptalk (jargon) in

the shop. In the shop, jargon is an excellent means of speeding up communication. One mechanic finds it a lot easier and faster to say to another mechanic, "Pass me the water pumps," instead of saying, "Pass me that pair of large, long-handled pliers." And lawyers talking to each other save a countless number of words by using terms such as "collateral estoppel" and "writ of mandamus."

Out of the shop, shoptalk is far less than useful. It is mystifying, confusing, fails to communicate, and can leave the impression that all the writer is trying to do is show off a supposedly vast amount of knowledge. This is unfortunate, for many specialized terms can be translated into plain English without splitting fine hairs of meaning. As examples:

Jargon	*Plain English*
hills of topographical heterogeneity	hills that are different
temporal and spatial differences	differences of time and space
strata	layers
neoplasm	tumor
arenaceous deposits	sand
riparian border	riverbank
littoral margin	shore
pyrexia	fever or elevated temperature
lesion	injury
cholelithiasis	gallstones
aestivate	dormant during summer

The use of jargon becomes even worse when an expression in one profession means something considerably different to the professional in another field, to say nothing of what the general reader thinks of such expressions. Consider these examples:

Force field analysis. To the electrical or electronics engineer, a *force field analysis* is an analysis of a magnetic field. To the planner or manager, a *force field analysis* is an analysis of the forces acting on a problem.

Secondary eco pack. A *secondary eco pack* can easily be taken to mean a "secondary life-support [*eco*] package" for an astronaut. Educators use *secondary eco pac* to refer to a package of educational materials for use in secondary school courses on the environment and ecology.

The chemical used for *vector* control is not DDT. (This sentence means nothing to the person who does not know that *vector* used in this sense means "pests" or "bugs." *Vector* has several, widely different meanings: a "force," a "line on a graph," a "direction an aircraft flies.")

The oral testimony at several points asserts that there is no substantial evidence for *chronic mortality*. (The phrase *chronic mortality* needs to be explained. As it stands, the sentence says "that there is no substantial evidence that death [mortality] lasts a long time [chronic].")

Alter ego. To the psychologist, or psychiatrist, the *alter ego* is another side of a person, a second self. To the lawyer, an *alter ego* is a sham corporation, a corporation in name only that is used for a fraudulent purpose.

Sidebar. To the newspaper or magazine editor, a *sidebar* is a short feature that accompanies the main story. To the lawyer, a *sidebar* is a conference between lawyers and the judge at the bench but outside the hearing of others in the court.

And these last examples bring us to the special problem of legal jargon.

TRANSLATIONS FROM THE LEGALESE

Law dominates many of the activities of business and government. This is as it should be. But does the language of lawyers—legalese—have to be so prevalent? Especially in view of the criticisms aimed at legalese?

Will Rogers: "Lawyers make a living out of trying to figure out what other lawyers have written." [2]

Abraham Lincoln, about a fellow lawyer: "He can compress the most words into the smallest idea of any man I ever met." [3]

Thomas Jefferson, in a letter to Joseph C. Cabell: "I dislike the verbose and intricate style of the English statutes, and in our revised code I endeavored to restore it to the simple one of the ancient statutes, in such original bills as I drew in that work. I suppose the information has not been acceptable, as it has been little followed. You, however, can easily correct this bill to the taste of my brother lawyers, by making every other word a 'said' or 'aforesaid,' and saying everything over two or three times, so that nobody but we of the craft can untwist the diction, and find out what it means." [4]

Jonathan Swift: "[Lawyers use] words multiplied for the purpose, . . . a peculiar cant and jargon of their own, that no other mortal can understand." [5]

Some mortals understand law language enough to know that it can be rewritten in a simpler form. In fact, the translation of legalese into plain English is the subject of several publications brought out beginning in the late 1970s. Among them are (and the following are also listed later in the section on additional reading): Rudolf Flesch's *How to Write Plain English: A Book for Lawyers and Consumers* (New York: Harper & Row, 1979); Janice C. Redish's "How to Write Regulations (and Other Legal Documents) in Clear English," in *Legal Notes and Viewpoints Quarterly*, August 1981; David Mellinkoff's *Legal Writing: Sense and Nonsense* (St. Paul, Minnesota: West Publishing, 1982); and Richard C. Wydick's *Plain English for Lawyers* (Durham, North Carolina: Carolina Academic Press, 1979). Both Mellinkoff and Wydick are attorneys. Mellinkoff is an authority on the history of the language of the law, and Wydick is a professor of law at the University of California, Davis.

In general, these publications cover the same topics as this book does: Write short sentences, use the specific word, use active-voice verbs, and so on. More specifically, the authors show how to convert legal jargon and phraseology into shorter, simpler forms while retaining the required meaning. One example is:

Legalese:
This being the case, the exclusionary clause can have no further force and effect, and full and complete relief can be given without the issuance of an injunction.
Rewritten:
In this case, the exclusionary clause has no further

effect, and complete relief can be given without issuing an injunction.

A minor change in the above sample was the shortening of the noun phrase "the issuance of" to a single verb, "issuing." More noteworthy was the reduction to one word of the redundant (needlessly repetitive) expressions "full and complete" and "force and effect."

Redundant expressions became popular with English-speaking lawyers centuries ago as English replaced French as the language of the law. Lawyers, in their concern to be precise, began using words from both languages. The habit has lasted to this day, with little or no justification. Accordingly, each of the redundancies listed below can be shortened to only one of the terms:

alter or change	full and complete
cease and desist	give, devise, and bequeath
convey, transfer, and set over	last will and testament
for and during the period	made and entered into
force and effect	null and void
free and clear	order and direct

The wise business writer also avoids writing out-of-date legalisms for which a more modern term can be used.

Out-of-date	Modern
aforementioned; aforesaid	mentioned earlier; mentioned previously
herein	here
hereinafter	later; after this

hereinbefore	earlier; before this
notwithstanding	regardless; in spite of
subsequent to	after

In this same category are the words *said, same,* and *such.* These words should not be used in place of *the,* for *the* is a more precise word.

In all, legal jargon should be avoided as much as possible. Legalese baffles and annoys nonlawyers and makes readers think a document is unreadable whether it is or not.

Translating legal jargon into plain English is one task facing the writer. Another task is that of recognizing that legal documents—laws, company regulations, or policy directives—cannot cover all bets. The Ten Commandments have withstood the test of time because they are terse. On the other hand, the classic example of a regulation that no one will pay any attention to is this one by a writer (or group of writers) in the National Park Service:

TREES, SHRUBS, PLANTS, GRASS AND OTHER VEGETATION

General Injury. No person shall prune, cut, carry away, pull up, dig, fell, bore, chop, saw, chip, pick, move, sever, climb, molest, take, break, deface, destroy, set fire to, burn, scorch, carve, paint, mark, or in any manner interfere with, tamper, mutilate, misuse, disturb or damage any tree, shrub, plant, grass, flower, or part thereof, nor shall any person permit any chemical, whether solid, fluid, or gaseous, to seep, drip, drain or be emptied, sprayed, dusted or injected upon, about or into any tree, shrub, plant, grass, flower, or part thereof except when specifically authorized by competent authority; nor shall any person build fires or station or use any tar kettle, heater, road roller or other engine within an area covered by this part in such a manner that the vapor, fumes or heat therefrom may injure any tree or other vegetation.[6]

All that says is: "Don't harm growing things," but when words are strung together in seemingly evident profusion, their meaning is not readily apparent.

Not all legal writing needs to be translated into plain English. An oft-quoted example of good writing is that of Benjamin Cardozo, late justice of the Supreme Court:

Plaintiff was standing on a platform of defendant's railroad after buying a ticket to go to Rockaway Beach. A train stopped at the station, bound for another place. Two men ran forward to catch it. One of the men reached the platform of the car without mishap, though the train was already moving. The other man, carrying a package, jumped aboard the car, but seemed unsteady as if about to fall. A guard on the car, who had held the door open, reached forward to help him in, and another guard on the platform pushed him from behind. In this act, the package was dislodged and fell upon the rails. It was a package of small size, about fifteen inches long, and was covered by a newspaper. In fact it contained fireworks, but there was nothing in its appearance to give notice of its contents. The fireworks when they fell exploded. The shock of the explosion threw down some scales at the other end of the platform many feet away. The scales struck the plaintiff, causing injuries for which she sues.[7]

Notice what distinguishes Justice Cardozo's style from that found in much legal writing. There is no out-of-date legal shoptalk, no *hereinbefores*. Most of the sentences are in active voice. Simple, specific words are used. Most sentences deal with only one main thought. The sentences are generally short, but provide variety by ranging in length from six to twenty-seven words. Ideas are closely and logically linked, and the passage moves right along—a well-written piece of narrative prose.

In all fairness to the writer, no right-thinking person expects specialists to write literature in which everything is made crystal clear to everyone. Readers who do not understand the intricacies of electron flow and integrated circuits have no right to a detailed explanation of how computers work. Similarly, nonlawyers should expect to be mystified by much of legal theory and practice.

But in all fairness *to the reader,* the place for shoptalk is only in the shop.

Use abbreviations with care

8

Advice on understanding the differences between acronyms and initialisms and abbreviations, using abbreviations, coining abbreviations, the special problems associated with Latin abbreviations. Plus an explanation of one of the earliest abbreviations, SPQR, and the different meanings of AEIOU.

Abbreviations have been around for a long time. In ancient Rome, SPQR stood for *Senatus Populusque Romanus,* "Senate and People of Rome." [1] A boastful inscription of the fifteenth century read AEIOU, *Austria Est Imperare Orbi Universo,* "It Is Given to Austria to Rule the Whole World." After Austria's losses in the war of 1866, jokesters added a new meaning to AEIOU: "Austria's Emperor Is Ousted Utterly." [2]

Today, abbreviations make up a new language that is increasingly popular with writers. The new language consists of approximately half a million abbreviations, which is roughly the same number of words as in the English language. This new language is defined in some twenty different dictionaries. The most comprehensive of these dictionaries is the *Acronyms, Initialisms, and Abbreviations Dictionary,* put out by the Gale Research

Company of Detroit. The 1980 edition of the Gale dictionary contains 211,000 entries, up from 12,000 in the first edition twenty years earlier.[3] Abbreviations are here to stay, despite the protests of those who decry them, and could well be the growth industry of language!

ACRONYMS, INITIALISMS, AND ABBREVIATIONS

As the title of the Gale dictionary says, abbreviations have company. The company consists of two subcategories of abbreviations: *acronyms* and *initialisms.*

An acronym is made up of the initial letters of an expression and is usually read or spoken as a word rather than letter by letter. The word *laser* (Light Amplification by Stimulated Emission of Radiation) is an acronym as is the U.S. Postal Service's *ZIP* (Zone Improvement Plan).

An initialism is also composed of the initial letters of an expression but is pronounced letter by letter rather than as a word. Examples of initialisms are *rpm* (revolutions per minute) and *GNP* (Gross National Product).

About the best definition left for an abbreviation is that it is a shortened form that is neither an acronym nor an initialism. Examples of abbreviations are *Dr.* (Doctor), *Calif.* (California), and *mb* (millibar).

Despite the growth in the number of abbreviations, they are unpopular with the reader who is unfamiliar with the term. Abbreviations are also unpopular with editors, indexers, researchers, translators, and typists. An English civil servant once wrote "by-laws concerned with h.w.c."—which the typist misread as "height of water closet [toilet]." The proper expression was "housing of the working classes." [4]

When using abbreviations, it is never safe to assume that readers or listeners know what's being discussed.

During the Apollo 12 space mission, controllers discovered a malfunction in a unit called the Digital Uplink Assembly. "We think we've figured it out," they radioed to the vicinity of the moon. "Your DUA was off." Replied the astronauts, who'd had years of training for the mission, "What is a DUA?" [5]

Deciphering an abbreviation is a special chore when one abbreviation can stand for a number of things in the same profession. Doctors, given to writing abbreviations on patients' records and having to read the same records, encounter *ID,* which stands for "intradermal" to the dermatologist, "inside diameter" to the physiologist, "ineffective dose" to the bacteriologist, and the more universal *idem* (the same). To a librarian, *CC* is used for the cataloguing system of "colon classification"; the publications *Christian Century, Comic Crusader, Cross Currents,* and *Current Contents;* and "carbon copy."

Undefined abbreviations are a source of trouble for both readers and writers. Readers may not understand or may misunderstand the abbreviation and respond in a different way from what the writer intended. Therefore:

• Spell out the term at first use and include the abbreviation in parentheses, as in Graduated Payment Mortgage (GPM).
• Provide a glossary if many abbreviations are used.
• Follow the golden rule of abbreviations: When in doubt, spell them out.

The following are several additional considerations governing the use of abbreviations:

• Write them as you would say them. "A registered nurse" becomes *"an* RN," not "a RN." The pronunciation is "an are-en."

- Don't drop articles (*a, an,* and *the*). If you would spell out "the Office of Administrative Law," then the abbreviation is written as "the OAL."
- Punctuated or unpunctuated? The trend is toward unpunctuated abbreviations, that is, no periods between the letters. As an example, EPA instead of E.P.A., for "Environmental Protection Agency."
- Capitalized or lowercased? Perhaps because of the influence of computer printouts, many abbreviations these days are written in all capital letters—BTU instead of Btu, for "British thermal unit."

Care should also be taken when coining abbreviations not to produce ones that are embarrassing. As examples: ACNE (Alaskans Concerned for Neglected Environments) and ACHE (Alabama Commission on Higher Education). Also, BARF (Best Available Retrofit Facility, a term used in air pollution control), SCAB (South Coast Air Basin, a California locale), and TART (Tahoe Area Regional Transit).

LATIN ABBREVIATIONS

Still another problem arises with the use of *e.g.* (*exempli gratia*) and *i.e.* (*id est*). These are Latin abbreviations, not English. The first, *e.g.*, is vague and means "for example"; *i.e.* is specific and means "that is." Few people know Latin these days, which is one reason not to use a Latin abbreviation. Another reason is to avoid mixing them up, a move that will confuse even the reader who does know Latin. Both of these sentences were found in the same document:

Space must be allotted on the form for routine personnel matters, *e.g.*, pay, vacation, sick leave, and insurance.

As was stated earlier, space must be allotted on the form for routine personnel matters, *i.e.,* pay, vacation, sick leave, and insurance.

The best procedure is to write out in English exactly what is meant: *for example* or *that is.*

A similar problem occurs with *etc.* (*et cetera*). Because writers have abused *etc.* so much, dictionaries have given it a variety of meanings: "and so forth," "and the like," "a number of unspecified additional persons or things," and "customary extras."

The impression often left by the use of *etc.* is that the writer (1) has no other way to cover up a lack of knowledge, (2) doesn't have the slightest idea of what to say next but feels that something should be said, or (3) wishes to produce some sort of idea of magnitude or multitude, as in this sample:

The value of this publication rests in its innate ability to communicate an understanding of the people's habits, needs, ideas, manners, etc.

The abbreviation *etc.* can be avoided by making lists and series as complete and as specific as possible. When an incomplete series must be written, it should be introduced with *for example, including,* or *such as;* and *etc.* should be omitted:

Instead of	*Write*
This publication covers the people's habits, needs, ideas, manners, *etc.*	This publication covers topics *such as* the people's habits, needs, ideas, and manners.

This may not seem like much of an improvement, but it does show that the writer was thinking before writing the series and not just idly tacking *etc.* onto the end.

Finally, there's not a lot of advice to give about abbreviations. They're here to stay. Use them, but use them with care.

Break up long sentences

9

Advice on breaking long sentences into short ones, eliminating unnecessary sentences, removing interruptions, breaking long sentences into lists, and the "magic number" of sentence length. *Plus* a tale of eighteenth-century England, complete with hero, heroine, and villain—told in what could be the world's longest sentence.

Here is a tale of eighteenth-century England, complete with hero, heroine, and villain:

And the said Edward by L.S. his attorney comes and defends the force and injury when &c. and as to the force and arms, the said Edward says, that he is not guilty thereof, as the said William Cooke above against him complains: And of this he puts himself on the Country [trial by jury]: And the said William Cooke thereof likewise: And as to the residue of the trespass aforesaid above supposed to be committed, the same Edward says, that the said William Cooke ought not to have this action against him, because he says, that one Laurence Jersey, at Tyley, otherwise Trinley aforesaid, before the said time when the trespass aforesaid is supposed to be committed, to wit, on the same 29th day of October in the year abovesaid, was possessed of three hogsheads of cyder, as of his own proper goods; and he the said Laurence being so as aforesaid possessed of the said three hogsheads of cyder, before the said time when, &c. to wit, on the same 29th day of October, at Tyley, otherwise Trinley, aforesaid, the same three hogsheads of cyder delivered to one Richard Baxter, to be safely kept, and from thence to Gloucester in the County of the same city to be carried; by virtue whereof the said Richard Baxter of the said three hogsheads of cyder was possessed: And farther the same Edward says that the said Richard Baxter being so as aforesaid of the said three hogsheads of cyder possessed, the said William Cooke at the said time when, &c. to wit, on the same 29th day of October abovesaid, at Tyley, otherwise Trinley aforesaid, the said three hogsheads of cyder from the possession and custody of the said R. Baxter would and endeavoured to take and carry away, and on one J. Baxter, the wife of the said R. Baxter, then and there the same three hogsheads of cyder for the same R. Baxter keeping, and the possession thereof preserving, then and there made an assault, and her then and there beat, wounded and abused; wherefore the same Edward, then and there being then the servant of the said Richard Baxter, as the servant of the said Richard Baxter, the said Jane, the wife of the said Richard Baxter his said master, and the possession of the said Richard Baxter his master of the said three hogsheads of cyder, lest the said W. Cooke should the said Jane farther hurt and overpower, and the said three hogsheads of cyder from the custody and possession of the said Richard Baxter, the said master of the said Edward, should take and carry away, and for the preservation of the possession of the said Richard Baxter, the said master of him the said Edward, of the said three hogsheads of cyder, against the said William Cooke did defend, as he lawfully might; and thereupon the said William Cooke on him the said Edward did then and there make an assault, and him the said Edward would have beat and abused, wherefore the same Edward did then and there defend himself against the said William Cooke; which is the same residue of the trespass whereof the said William above thereof now complains; and so the same Edward says that the injury or damage, if any, then and there happened to the same William Cooke, it arose from the proper assault of him the said William Cooke, and in defence of the said Jane, the wife of the said Richard Baxter, the master of him the said Edward, and of the possession of the said Richard Baxter, the master of him the said Edward, of the said three hogsheads of Cyder, and in defence of him the said Edward: And this same Edward is ready to verify: Wherefore he prays judgment if the said William Cooke ought to have his action aforesaid against him, &c.[1]

One sentence. Did you struggle through it? And if you did, do you know what it was about? It was an attorney's pleading, written in the legal language of the time.

Stripped of repetition and unnecessary words and broken into short sentences, the same story can be told in this form:

Laurence Jersey delivered three hogsheads of cider to Richard Baxter. William Cooke, the villain, tried to steal the cider. Jane, Richard's wife and the heroine, interfered, and Cooke started to beat her up. Enter the hero, Edward, servant to the Baxters. Edward and William Cooke fought it out, and Edward rescued Jane and saved the cider. Cooke, scoundrel that he was, took Edward to court and charged him with assault. Edward entered a plea that his actions were justified.

BREAKING LONG SENTENCES INTO SHORT ONES

The standard advice in books on how to write is this: Write short sentences. That's fine, for people who instinctively know how to write short sentences.

But what about the rest of us, those whose every sentence comes out long? What do we do? Answer: We write the long sentence, and then we edit it into shorter ones, which is one of the easiest tasks that a writer faces. As a starting point, consider this sentence:

The Control Evaluation Section, consisting of four Environmental Health Specialists, is responsible for maintaining the agency's list of major pollutant sources and for operating the statewide upset-maintenance activity tracking system which includes logging incoming information, entering computer data, and evaluating upset-maintenance incidents for possible enforcement actions.

Rewrite #1. The easiest thing to do is retain the original sequence of ideas while breaking up the sentence into smaller ones:

The Control Evaluation Section consists of four Environmental Health Specialists. The section is responsible for maintaining the agency's list of major pollutant sources and for operating the statewide upset-maintenance activity tracking system. The section's tasks include logging incoming information, entering computer data, and evaluating upset-maintenance incidents for possible enforcement actions.

Rewrite #2. The first rewrite lacks polish, for all the sentences begin with *the.* To improve, leave the first two sentences as they stand, and rewrite the third sentence to begin:

Tasks performed by the section include logging incoming information, entering computer data, and evaluating upset-maintenance incidents for possible enforcement actions.

Another long sentence that can be broken into shorter, more readable sentences is this one:

Employees in a class shall receive a salary within the limits established for that class; provided, that when a position has been allocated to a lower class or when the salary of the class is reduced, the department may authorize the payment of a rate above the maximum of the class; and provided further, that when an employee is moved to a lower class because of reductions in force or other management-initiated changes, the department may authorize the payment of a rate above the maximum of the class to the employee whose service has been fully satisfactory and who has completed a minimum of 10 years of service.

That long-winded monster can be rewritten as:

(1) Employees in a class shall receive a salary within the limits established for that class. (2) This limitation does not apply when a position has been allocated to a lower class or when the salary of the class is reduced. (3) In those instances, the depart-

ment may authorize the payment of a rate above the maximum of the class. (4) In addition, salary limits established for a class do not apply when an employee is moved to a lower class because of reductions in force or other management-initiated changes. (5) In those instances, the department also may authorize the payment of a rate above the maximum of the class. (6) The above-maximum rate is authorized for an employee whose service has been fully satisfactory and who has completed a minimum of 10 years of service.

In the rewritten version, two sentences, 3 and 5, carry the same thought. By eliminating one of the sentences, the sample is shortened even more:

(1) Employees in a class shall receive a salary within the limits established for that class. (2) This limitation does not apply when a position has been allocated to a lower class or when the salary of the class is reduced. (3) In addition, salary limits established for a class do not apply when an employee is moved to a lower class because of reductions in force or other management-initiated changes. (4—old 3 & 5) Whenever salary limitations do not apply, the department may authorize the payment of a rate above the maximum. (5—old 6) The above-maximum rate is authorized for an employee whose service has been fully satisfactory and who has completed a minimum of 10 years of service.

REMOVING INTERRUPTIONS

Another way to break up a long sentence is to take out the interrupting or parenthetical elements and place them elsewhere. Note this before-and-after combination and the repositioning of the italicized interruption:

Before

The Control Evaluation Section, *consisting of four Environmental Health Specialists,* is responsible for maintaining the agency's list of major pollutant sources.

After

The Control Evaluation Section is responsible for maintaining the agency's list of major pollutant sources. *Four Environmental Health Specialists make up the section's staff.*

Another example is this piece of legal writing. Again, the interrupting element is shown in italics:

The prohibition of this section does not apply to the federal government or any agency thereof or any law enforcement agency, *other than a fire agency,* of the state government of any agency or local subdivision thereof, including counties, cities, districts, authorities, and agencies.

This sentence becomes easier to read if rewritten as:

The prohibition of this section applies to fire agencies. This prohibition does not apply to the federal government or any agency thereof or any law enforcement agency of the state government or any agency or local subdivision thereof, including counties, cities, districts, authorities, and agencies.

BREAKING LONG SENTENCES INTO LISTS

Sometimes the shortest, clearest way to present a complicated piece of material is to put it into a list, which is also known as a *tabulation* or *outline style*. Consider this long sentence, which contains several provisions:

> Solvent producers are qualified for exemptions if they produce fewer than 50 gallons of solvent per day, are ranked in the lower one-third of income groupings for their standard industrial classification, transport fewer than 25 gallons of solvent per day off of their plant sites, operate their manufacturing processes fewer than nine hours per day for a five-day work week or in any event no more than 45 hours in any one calendar week, and are engaged primarily in the business of solvent production for individual hobbyists.

The provisions listed in that sentence would be a lot easier to find if arranged in a vertical list:

> Solvent producers are qualified for exemptions if they:
>
> a. Produce fewer than 50 gallons of solvent per day;
>
> b. Are ranked in the lower one-third of income groupings for their standard industrial classification;
>
> c. Transport fewer than 25 gallons of solvent per day off of their plant sites;
>
> d. Operate their manufacturing processes fewer than nine hours per day for a five-day work week or in any event no more than 45 hours in any one calendar week; and

e. Are engaged primarily in the business of solvent production for individual hobbyists.

Notice these features of a list:

1. Items are indented to set them off from material placed before and after.

2. Items are of the same class. Putting exemption requirements into a list with reporting requirements would be wrong, just as it would be wrong to write a list consisting of apples, supersonic airliners, and llama drivers.

3. Each item begins with a capital letter. This is not always necessary. Multiple choice test items need not be capitalized unless they are proper nouns:

| 1. tables | a. Romeo and Juliet |
| 2. chairs | b. five-act play |

In addition, short items are often not capitalized:

geology
meteorology
petrology
paleontology

4. Long items have ending punctuation. If a long item is part of a sentence, the ending punctuation is a semicolon. When a list is made up of long items separated by semicolons, the ending punctuation for the last item is a period. If a long item can stand alone as a sentence, the ending punctuation is a period. Short items in a vertical list need not have ending punctuation.

5. In a list with items separated by semicolons, the last two items are joined by *and* or *or,* depending upon conditions established for the list.

6. A list is usually introduced with a colon, although a dash (—) can be used in place of the colon. No punctua-

tion is needed to introduce or end the list if the introductory sentence flows smoothly into the list:

The topics of the lectures were
> geology
> meteorology
> petrology
> paleontology

7.   A period without parentheses is used after numerals or letters used to enumerate items in a vertical list.

8. Numerals or letters are used to enumerate items when items must be accomplished in order or when the need for cross-references might arise. Otherwise, items can be called out with a bullet, which is a filled-in dot (•).

When writing short sentences, there is no magic number of words to shoot for. An *average* sentence length of fifteen to twenty words is a good figure for reaching the vast majority of readers. This estimate comes from approximately a hundred readability studies performed during the last half-century. Nevertheless, readability studies do not measure factors such as word meaning, word order, words omitted, awkward constructions, and misused words.

Therefore, it is very easy and very correct to say that a short sentence can contain more nonsense than a long one. In that case, the overriding requirement can be stated quite simply: Make all sentences clear regardless of length.

Write time-saving paragraphs

10

Advice on paragraph topic sentences, supporting the topic sentence, transitions within the paragraph, connecting one paragraph to the next, and the "magic number" of paragraph length.

Can you imagine what it would be like to read an entire book that consisted of one long paragraph? How could you tell where the author introduced a new topic? Think what the page would look like—solid masses of words without a break.

Well, if you had lived four centuries ago, that's what kind of pages you would have seen, for the indented paragraph did not come into use until the seventeenth century.[1] And if you see paragraphs in a recent edition of a book written before then, the paragraphing has been supplied by a modern-day editor.

Paragraphs today come in several forms. Newspapers often use one-sentence paragraphs to present a story in short bursts. Magazines such as *The New Yorker* follow a style that calls for long, highly developed paragraphs. Writers of dialogue start a new paragraph when a different character begins to speak. In fiction, the story is advanced and action is shown in a narrative paragraph, a paragraph that is nothing more than a very short story.

THE TIME-SAVING PARAGRAPH

In business writing, the paragraph style most commonly used is one that saves time for the busy reader. This saving is brought about by introducing the topic of the paragraph in the first sentence. When a paragraph is written in this manner, the reader can skim the first sentence and then decide whether to read the entire paragraph or move on to the next one.

When this procedure is *not* followed, the reader must often plow through the entire paragraph to learn what the subject is. As an example, the paragraph below lacks a key ingredient, a sentence to introduce it:

> A survey returned by 1,367 graduates of the class of 1981 showed that the median salary of these graduates was $20,330. These former students said that their college experience had made strong contributions to their understanding of written information and scientific methods and principles; to their abilities to make logical inferences and reach correct conclusions; to their abilities to define and solve problems; and to their self-confidence and self-understanding.

After readers have gone through the paragraph, they could guess that it has something to do with the value of a college education. They would also have a right to ask: What is the connection between salary (first sentence) and the information in the rest of the paragraph?

But why should readers play guessing games? Why make the reader ask questions? Instead, make the reader's task easier by adding a *topic sentence,* a sentence at the start of the paragraph to tell the reader what the paragraph is about:

> *What is the value of a college education?* A survey returned by 1,367 graduates of the class of 1981

showed . . . These former students said that their college experience had made strong contributions to their . . .

Incidentally, writing paragraphs in this manner also saves time for the writer if it is necessary to add headings, for the heading can easily be extracted from the first sentence of the paragraph. As an example, note how the italicized words in the first sentence:

What is *the value of a college education?* A survey returned . . .

become a heading:

The value of a college education
   What is the value of a college education? A survey returned . . .

When headings and paragraph first sentences echo each other, this repetition aids the reader in learning and remembering the material.

REQUIREMENTS FOR A WELL-WRITTEN PARAGRAPH

A well-written paragraph begins with a *topic sentence,* contains material that *supports* the topic, and is held together with verbal *glue.* More information on these items is as follows:

1. *A topic sentence*—a sentence that introduces the subject of the paragraph. The topic sentence should be the first sentence in the paragraph. The topic sentence is the most general in the paragraph.

2. *Support*—material used to develop or explain the idea introduced in the topic sentence. Support material

consists of evidence, facts, details, specific information, opinions, and examples.

3. *Glue*—words that connect one idea to the next. Glue consists of transitional words and phrases such as *moreover* or *in addition* and terms that repeat or echo key ideas.

All three of these items are used in the paragraph below. The sentences are numbered for later reference.

(1) With respect to women, a concerted affirmative action effort began more recently, but today stands on an equal footing with the efforts being made on behalf of minorities. (2) It is encouraging to note the significantly increased number of women, particularly in management positions and as professionals and sales workers. (3) Between 1968 and 1976, the number of women officials and managers has more than tripled, the number of women professionals has increased by well over 100% and the number of women sales workers has increased from a total of six to a total of 119 as of March, 1976.[2]

1. *Topic sentence.* Sentence 1 is the topic sentence. It announces the topic of the paragraph—affirmative action for women. The topic sentence also contains the phrases "more recently" and "equal footing," both very general terms.

2. *Support.* Sentence 2 begins the development of this paragraph's support material. The specific information Sentence 2 provides is that an increasing number of women work in management, professional, and sales positions. Sentence 3 increases the amount of support by providing very detailed information—the years 1968 and 1976, the phrases "more than tripled" and "increased by

well over 100%," and the specific example, "increased from a total of six to a total of 119."

3. *Glue.* One form of glue is easy to spot, the word *women.* That word is used in each sentence. Another form of glue is that of *increase.* The increase is described in general terms in sentence 1, and sentences 2 and 3 specifically use the word *increased.* The idea of *increase* is echoed throughout the paragraph.

The paragraph just studied dealt with factual material. The next paragraph shows how to develop an argument for an abstract point.

> (1) Many observers of the Washington scene have felt for some time that our nation lacked a cohesive foreign economic policy. (2) Traditionally, many of our economic relationships with other nations seem to have been dominated and dictated by foreign policy considerations of a military or political nature. (3) Many also feel that our policymakers have not been attuned or responsive to the realities and changes occurring over the years in the international economic arena. (4) Instead, our policymakers seem to meet current problems by going to the shelf and dusting off old policies, without either sufficient regard for their current relevancy or sufficient analysis of the long-term ramifications of their implementation.[3]

1. *Topic sentence.* Sentence 1 is the topic sentence. It announces the subject of the paragraph—lack of a cohesive foreign economic policy. Sentence 1 also contains the general terms "Many observers" and "for some time."

2. *Support.* Sentences 2, 3, and 4 contain this paragraph's support. Sentence 2 argues that the problems with our foreign economic policy are caused by military

and political considerations. Sentence 3 says that the problems with foreign economic problems are caused by inattentive policymakers. According to sentence 4, the problem is that policymakers rely on old, out-dated policies.

Sentences 2, 3, and 4 are general statements not backed up by facts. Factual support for this paragraph would have included the naming of specific instances where foreign economic policy had failed because of reasons cited in the paragraph.

3. *Glue.* The glue in this paragraph is of two types. The echo type consists of the words *foreign economic policy* (sentence 1); *economic relationships, other nations,* and *foreign policy* (sentence 2); *international economic arena* (sentence 3); and *policymakers* and *policies* (sentence 4). This paragraph also uses the transitional words *Traditionally* (sentence 2), *also* (sentence 3), and *Instead* (sentence 4).

USING TRANSITIONS

Transitions are a form of verbal glue that are relatively easy to use and make the reader's task considerably easier. A transition is a word or group of words placed early in the sentence:

Without transitions	*With transitions*
One such possibility uses the so-called solar sail. Solar radiation is used to drive a spacecraft on a complex, four-year orbit to a rendezvous with Halley's comet near perihelion in early 1986.	One such possibility uses the so-called solar sail. *In this method,* solar radiation is used ...

The number of orders has doubled in the past six months. The department staff must be increased. Training must be provided and qualified applicants notified.	The number of orders has doubled in the past six months. *Therefore,* the department staff must be increased. *In addition,* training must be provided, and qualified applicants notified.

Note: In the second sentence, do not write, "The department staff must *therefore* be increased." A transition works best if placed early in the sentence, to carry the reader from one idea to the next.

CONNECTING ONE PARAGRAPH TO THE NEXT

Besides using glue to hold a paragraph together internally, glue should also be used to connect one paragraph to the next. To do so develops continuity, so important for keeping the reader moving through the whole piece of writing. Note how the three paragraphs below are held together:

Edwin Newman, of the National Broadcasting Company, gave the keynote address. Newman both amused and horrified his audience with examples of pompous and illiterate language from government documents, business writing, newspapers, sports reporting, television commercials, and other sources. The diversity of Newman's examples shows how pervasive gobbledygook is in our society.

Enough is never enough, said Newman, for people who have to "pre-plan" before they can begin or for people who "affirmatively approve" a proposal. In today's business world, people aren't fired; they are "outplaced." Companies don't subcontract; they "outsource." You might need a translator to understand that when the weatherman predicts an end to the current "precipitation regime," he means that it will stop raining or to realize that if you are "transportation disadvantaged," you don't own a car.

As Newman pointed out, pompous and obscure language like this is dull and ineffective. It is also often wrong. Is incorrect English really necessary, Newman asked, to sell products on television? Wouldn't beer and jeans sell as well if advertisers used pronouns correctly and didn't use "good" as an adverb?[4]

What connects one paragraph to the next? One word: *Newman,* used in the topic sentence of each paragraph.

It is also possible to connect paragraphs with a transitional word or phrase. The two paragraphs below are connected by the word *unfortunately.*

Managers of all types of organizations, both public and private, need feedback to guide future decisions regarding continuation or modification of their organization's activities.

Unfortunately, too many state and local governments lack the feedback necessary to measure program effectiveness. There is little basis for judging whether a specific program is working as planned and, equally important, how well it is serving the public. Information, where it exists, usually is sketchy and inadequate for decision making.[5]

PARAGRAPH LENGTH

Finally, there is the problem of length. How long should a paragraph be? No pat answer exists. It is dead wrong to make arbitrary and baseless rules such as five lines long, five sentences long, or no longer than a dollar bill is wide. Writers who follow such rules, and some do, have forgotten that the purpose of a paragraph is to cover a topic, not so much space on a page. What should be done instead is to write up the topic adequately but don't make the paragraph so long that the reader will get lost in it or not even want to read it in the first place.

Get to the point

11

Advice on why writers turn out mystery stories, how readers benefit when the main idea is placed early in a piece of writing, and the fact that placing the main idea early is merely a matter of cut-and-paste. *Plus* this thought: If you have something important to say, the last place to put it is the last place.

Why do writers take so long to get to the point? Why do drafts and many final versions read like mystery stories—where you plod through page after page until you get to the information you need to know?

One reason is timidity. The writer is reluctant to get to the point until everything else is said. Another reason, perhaps the most predominant, is tradition, a tradition that can be traced back to the philosopher Aristotle.

More than two thousand years ago Aristotle lectured on what we would now call "Effective Public Speaking." Over the centuries, these lectures became known as Aristotle's *Rhetoric*. The *Rhetoric* is packed with ideas and observations about what goes into a good speech, including what Aristotle had to say about organization. In brief, Aristotle proposed that a speech contain an introduction, narrative, and arguments that lead to a concluding or ending main statement.[1] Because Aristotle was dealing with speeches as opposed to the printed word, anyone wanting to be sure of the main idea had to wait around until the end.

The similarities between speaking and writing are many. Therefore, when writing began to be taught, teachers adopted much of Aristotle's *Rhetoric*. They included Aristotle's way of organizing a speech and made it standard fare in composition courses. Many writers of scientific and technical material find Aristotle's method attractive, for it closely parallels the inductive method of accumulating, recording, and analyzing observations before writing down conclusions. In science, inductively organized writing is a product of long-standing tradition, and it is a tradition followed by writers in many fields in addition to science.

For more than three-quarters of a century, researchers have been questioning the traditional inductive pattern of writing. The question asked is: Does the reader benefit most from the inductive method (main idea last) or from the deductive method (main idea first)? The studies have concentrated almost solely on nonfiction, informative prose, and the most thoroughly supported and documented findings are:

• Readers remember information in greater depth if the information appears early in a written passage rather than later.

• Readers remember information longer if the information appears early in a written passage rather than later.

• Difficulty of learning increases as the length of a written passage increases.

*   *   *

In addition, some evidence exists that arguments presented early in a piece of writing are more persuasive than arguments presented later. Finally, a researcher measuring 14,652 individual reading habits of the newspaper-reading general public arrived at the conclusion that as a piece of writing gets longer, less of it will be read, and it will lose readers.[2]

This is all very well and good, but how do we do it? How do we take our research and our thinking, which are done inductively, and turn them into a deductively organized piece of writing?

Simple. While we're doing the research, we write it up inductively. Before it's time to have the writing typed in final form, we get out the scissors and tape and cut and paste until we have a deductively organized presentation.

As an example, consider this problem that was handed to a personnel analyst:

Subject: Assignment of newly created Housing Specialist I and II classifications.

Question: Union representatives have asked whether a person hired as a Housing Specialist I or II should be assigned to our administrative unit or to the enforcement unit.

In researching the problem, the analyst wrote these three findings:

1. According to the specification sheet for the class, Housing Specialists I and II perform duties that are largely advisory, analytical, and developmental. Our administrative unit is made up of other classes in which the duties are also largely advisory, analytical, and developmental.

2. The enforcement duties of Housing Specialists

I and II are mentioned in only a small portion of the specification sheet for those classes. It would therefore seem that the positions are not primarily of an enforcement nature and should not be assigned to the enforcement unit.

3. If enforcement duties were the criteria for evaluating a position, most other classes in the organization would be assigned to the enforcement unit. As an example, all of our engineers have some enforcement duties, yet the primary skills and duties of these engineers have led to their being placed in units other than enforcement.

Conclusion. Therefore, Housing Specialists I and II should be assigned to the administrative unit.

The last thing arrived at was the answer: Housing Specialists I and II belong in the administrative unit. But note where that answer is placed in the final version:

Subject: Assignment of newly created Housing Specialist I and II classifications.

Question: Union representatives have asked whether a person hired as a Housing Specialist I or II should be assigned to our administrative unit or to the enforcement unit.

Answer: Administrative unit. My reasons are:

1. According to the specification sheet for the class, Housing Specialists I and II perform duties that are largely advisory, analytical, and developmental. Our administrative unit is made up of other classes in which the duties are also largely advisory, analytical, and developmental.

2. The enforcement duties of Housing Specialists I and II are mentioned in only a small portion of the specification sheet for those classes. It

would therefore seem that the positions are not primarily of an enforcement nature and should not be assigned to the enforcement unit.

3. If enforcement duties were the criteria for evaluating a position, most other classes in the organization would be assigned to the enforcement unit. As an example, all of our engineers have some enforcement duties, yet the primary skills and duties of these engineers have led to their being placed in units other than enforcement.

The long and short of getting to the point is that it is a task of reorganization. It is a task of first writing the document in a form that is most convenient for the writer, and then reorganizing the writing to serve the reader. The reorganization can be done with scissors and tape or with word processing equipment. However it is done, it must accomplish this purpose: Serve the reader.

A REPORT FOR STUDY

Serving the reader becomes especially important with a long piece of writing such as a report. Business and technical reports easily run several hundred pages in length, and many fill volumes. Much of this length is given over to detailed descriptions of research methods and materials. Also contained within this length are explanations and analyses of findings or results—what was learned, measured or observed during the research. In addition, most reports present conclusions, that is, logical assumptions based on the results of the research. Moreover, many reports offer recommendations, suggested courses of action that follow naturally from the conclusions.

Hand something that bulky and complex to a busy person, and you can expect to get these reactions: "Do you expect me to read all that?" "What's really so important about this report?" "What's in it for me?"

Writers have devised ways to answer those questions quickly. One way is to use an abstract, a paragraph or two placed in front of the report to present the report's highlights—the results, conclusions, and recommendations. In some cases a brief summary is placed in front of the report; the purpose of the summary is the same as the purpose of the abstract—to give readers quick access to report highlights. In other cases the highlights are written into the report's introduction or presented in a section immediately after the introduction. In still other cases writers use combinations of the methods just described.

Regardless of the method used, the general organizational pattern is this: Highlights are presented up front, and research methods and materials are described later in the report.

An example is the report *Child Care Initiatives for Working Parents: Why Employers Get Involved,* published by the American Management Associations.[3] This well-written report is about the size of a book slightly smaller than the average hardcover book. The report consists of an introduction, six chapters, two appendixes, and a list of reference material. Conclusions arrived at in the six chapters are brought forward and presented in the introduction. I have divided my description of the report into sections on its introduction, its main body (the six chapters), and the back matter (the appendixes and list of references). Sections of the report have been edited to control length.

Report introduction. To establish a relationship to the report's title, *Child Care Initiatives for Working Par-*

ents, the introduction begins with general statements about the increasing need for child care. These general statements are followed with specific ones that are called to the reader's attention with bullets, as in the list below:

- One-third of all mothers with infants work.
- Women are returning to work within six weeks to three months after childbirth, leaving infants in some kind of child care arrangement.
- Almost 66 percent of all husband-wife families now have two earners.
- Sixty-six percent of all single (separated, divorced, widowed, never-married) mothers are in the labor force.
- Forty-three percent of mothers with children under the age of three are in the labor force.
- Two-thirds of all working mothers leave their children with other adults for a significant part of the day. . . .

To establish a relationship to the report's subtitle, *Why Employers Get Involved,* the introduction also contains this language:

In the face of sweeping changes, employers accustomed to a traditional male labor force are finding it increasingly difficult to insulate themselves from family issues and the concerns of parent-employees. On the one hand, these employers realize that if their organizations (and the nation as a whole) are to utilize the available pool of talented workers, parent-employees must continue as working members of society. On the other hand, if employers are to adopt new work policies in response to child care needs, then it is important that they have information that will aid them in this crucial decision-making process. In many cases, the needed information is unavailable, incomplete, or inadequate. Issues and concerns such as these gave impetus to the present study.

The introduction's next part, "The Study—Its Focus and Goals," describes the design of the research:

The overall purpose of the study was to determine the current status and perceived benefits of employer initiatives for child care in the United States. More specifically, the survey was designed to provide data that would answer these questions:

1. How many child care programs are currently in operation? What kinds of organizations are sponsoring these programs?
2. What were the employers' reasons for initiating the programs?
3. What effects, from the employers' point of view, do these programs have on their organizations?
4. What benefits do employers see as growing out of these programs?
5. What do such programs cost? What financing arrangements did the sponsoring organizations use to establish the program?
6. How extensively do parent-employees use these programs?
7. What are the important features of the programs? . . .

Answers to those questions are given in the introduction's next section. Bold capital letters label the section, and individual items are called out with bullets.

HIGHLIGHTS and CONCLUSIONS

The survey data point to a heightened interest in child care incentives, considerable creativity and resourcefulness in the development of these incentives, and a recognition that both parents and employers benefit from an effective child care program. Consider these representative findings:

- The implementation of child care incentives has escalated in recent years. Of the 204 programs surveyed, 52 percent were established within the past five years.
- Service industries, such as banking, finance, insurance, and health care are the most responsive in providing child care services; of these, the health care organizations account for the largest portion of programs offered. The service industries have traditionally employed large numbers of female workers. The continuation of this practice, plus the record number of women now working, may well account for this phenomenon.
- Child care initiatives are found in organizations of all sizes. Sixty-nine of the 204 programs studied were in organizations with fewer than 1,500 employees; 10 programs were located in companies with fewer than 150 workers. . . .

Seven additional highlights and conclusions are given in this section of the introduction.

From there, the introduction goes on to summarize the major findings of the report. That is, child care services provided by employers benefit both the employer and the family:

A growing number of organizations have created initiatives toward the implementation of child care programs for working parents, thus helping to reduce the potential conflict between work and family. In reducing the conflict, employers may look forward to recruiting the best available pool of talented workers, retaining valuable and qualified personnel, reducing absenteeism, and developing a pool of more satisfied employees, thus improving the quality of worklife.

The survey data reveal that these goals, when accomplished, create a synergism that achieves the more basic goal cited by employers for establishing child care initiatives—a more stable workforce.

The relationship of motivation and perceived benefit to the organization is significant. Employers can fulfill management's agenda (creating a talented, stable workforce) while meeting the needs of working parents.

The introduction also contains a brief list of definitions used in the report. The placing of definitions or a glossary in the front of a report is wise, for readers will notice it there as they start through the report. To place definitions or a glossary in back is the same as placing it where readers may never see it.

Report main body. The report's main body consists of six chapters that describe research methods and develop the highlights and conclusions that are summarized in the introduction.

Chapter 1 summarizes the history of child care. Efforts in the federal and private sectors are covered. Much of this material is summarized as background information in the introduction.

Chapter 2 describes the means used to gather information on the current status of child care. In other words, chapter 2 tells how the author went about gathering information to take the subject of child care from the historical perspective to the perspective of the present.

Chapters 3 through 6 cover current information arrived at during the author's research. This information includes findings on who provides child care facilities, who uses them, what the cost is, and how employers benefit. Much of this material is treated in condensed form in the introduction.

Report back matter. The back matter consists of two appendixes and a list of references. One appendix is the survey questionnaire used to gather data. The second appendix is the cover letter sent with the survey questionnaire. As for the reference list, it is organized like the bibliographies found in many books.

Overall, the organization of *Child Care Initiatives for Working Parents* is fairly standard. The author arrived at the main body by first surveying the historical perspective, by then devising a means of gathering current information, and lastly by analyzing that current information. That was the method, but readers are more interested in results. Consequently, the author extracted pertinent results and placed them up front where they can be found more readily. Busy readers interested only in highlights and conclusions need not read past the introduction. Readers wanting more detail will proceed into the main body, and readers wanting still more information can check the appendixes and references.

This is not to say that every document must be organized in this manner. How-to-do-it instructions certainly don't fit into this mold, for they must be organized into a rigid, step-by-step sequence. Neither do bad-news letters or letters that say no. These letters, which are covered elsewhere in this book, use an indirect approach to lead up to the important points at the end, and that pattern or organization rightfully violates the principle of organization taught in this chapter.

Consequently, the organization of a piece of writing must be made to serve the purpose of the writing and the needs of the reader. Nevertheless, for most business and technical writing—reports, letters, and memos—organizational problems can be solved by remembering this advice: If you have something important to say, the last place to put it is the last place.

Vary your style

12

Advice on varying your writing
style to suit the situation, writing
"yes" and "no" letters, being
direct and forceful, when there's
no need to be direct and forceful,
and writing the personal memo
versus the policy memo. *Plus*
samples of different styles from
Mark Twain and the Japanese
school of letter writing.

An earlier chapter contained a quote by Mark Twain that commented on the misuse of facts. This chapter begins with two letters by Twain, writing under his real name of Samuel Langhorne Clemens. Each letter was written in a different style.

In the first letter, Twain dealt with a couple of serious issues by using humor. One issue was that of his dissatisfaction with copyright laws; the second issue was the banning of *Huckleberry Finn,* the book Twain mentioned. If it is possible to use simple terms when describing a subject as complex as humor, it might be said that the humor in this letter is good-natured and gentle.

TO FRANK A. NICHOLS, SECRETARY,
CONCORD FREE TRADE CLUB

Hartford, March, 1885.

Dear Sir:

I am in receipt of your favor of the 24th inst., conveying the gratifying intelligence that I have been made an honorary member of the Free Trade Club of Concord, Massachusetts, and I desire to express to the Club, through you, my grateful sense of the high compliment thus paid me.

It does look as if Massachusetts were in a fair way to embarrass me with kindnesses this year. In the first place a Massachusetts Judge has just decided in open court that a Boston publisher may sell not only his own property in a free and unfettered way, but may also as freely sell property which does not belong to him but to me— property which he has not bought and which I have not sold. Under this ruling I am now advertising that judge's homestead for sale; and if I make as good a sum out of it as I expect I shall go on and sell the rest of his property.

In the next place, a committee of the public library of your town has condemned and excommunicated my last book, and doubled its sale. This generous action of theirs must necessarily benefit me in one or two additional ways. For instance, it will deter other libraries from buying the book and you are doubtless aware that one book in a public library prevents the sale of a sure ten and a possible hundred of its mates. And secondly it will cause the purchasers of the book to read it, out of curiosity, instead of merely intending to do so after the usual way of the world and library committees; and then they will discover, to my great advantage and their own indignant disappointment, that there is nothing objectionable in the book, after all.

And finally, the Free Trade Club of Concord comes forward and adds to the splendid burden of obligations already conferred upon me by the Commonwealth of Massachusetts, an honorary membership which is more worth than all the rest since it endorses me as worthy to associate with certain gentlemen whom even the moral icebergs of the Concord library committee are bound to respect.

May the great Commonwealth of Massachusetts endure forever, is the heartfelt prayer of one who, long a recipient of her mere general good will, is proud to realize that he is at last become her pet.

Thanking you again, dear sir and gentlemen, I remain

Your obliged servant
S. L. Clemens
(known to the Concord   Winter School of Philosophy as "Mark Twain.")[1]

In this next letter, Twain was anything but good-natured and gentle. Instead, given the times he lived in, he was downright unprintable.

TO THE GAS COMPANY

Hartford, February 12, 1891.

Dear Sirs:

Some day you will move me almost to the verge of irritation by your chuckle-headed Goddamned fashion of shutting your Goddamned gas off without giving any notice to your Goddamned parishioners. Several times you have come within an ace of smothering half of this house-

hold in their beds and blowing up the other half by this idiotic, not to say criminal, custom of yours. And it has happened again to-day. Haven't you a telephone?

Ys
S L Clemens[2]

What Twain did is what any good writer does—vary the style to suit the situation. No single style will work in all situations. Sometimes it's correct to be forceful and direct, and sometimes it's not. Sometimes it's correct to be friendly and personal, and sometimes the personal touch is inappropriate.

To put it bluntly, the writer's individual style is secondary to serving the purposes of the writing, to serving the purposes of the reader, and to serving the purposes of the organization.

When it comes to solving problems of style, one of the easiest of such problems is that of letters that present a neutral position, offer help, or say yes. People like to receive good news and to have their problems solved for them; witness the success of "Dear Abby" and "Dear Ann Landers." Accordingly, the neutral or "yes" business letter is relatively easy to write and should be organized to get to the point as quickly as possible. As an example:

Dear ————:

In response to your letter of August 9, 19—, Capitol City TV Repair, 419 Jefferson Boulevard, telephone 333–7777, is our authorized service center in your city. They will be pleased to adjust the video cassette recorder as you requested.

There will be no charge for this service.

If you have any further problems with the recorder,

please let us know. It's our newest model, and we want it to provide the entertainment you expect from it.

Sincerely,

On the other hand, the most difficult letter to receive and to write is the letter that says no. No one likes to be told no, and "no" letters can be charged with emotion. Unless the "no" letter is carefully prepared, the reader may be offended. And offensive letters are bad for business, as is this one:

Dear ————:

Small Appliance Manufacturing Corporation is unable to make the repairs requested on the vacuum cleaner shipped to us, model 6983a, serial #4157831.

The warranty on this appliance expired three months ago. In addition, it appears that someone has tampered with the wiring and caused the problems described.

Accordingly, the appliance is being returned.

Sincerely,

The stylistic faults in the above letter are:

1. *Improper organization.* The letter opens with the "no" answer, a beginning that is coldhearted and too direct. Instead, the facts and reasons should be presented early in the letter to lead the reader to the "no" answer at or near the end. This indirect approach is softer and helps ensure that the reader reads the entire letter and understands the logic behind the "no" answer. The typical "no" letter violates the principle of getting to the point early in a piece of writing.

2. *Accusatory in nature.* The sentence about tampering

with the wiring is unnecessary. The wiring may have been damaged when the vacuum cleaner was manufactured, and the damaged wiring may not in fact have caused the problems described. Moreover, the so-called damaged wiring is not the reason the factory won't make the repairs; the expired warranty is the only pertinent reason for not making the repairs.

3. *Cold, formal approach.* This letter lacks personal pronouns such as *you, I, we,* and *us*—the little words that make a letter sound as if one human wrote to another human. In addition, the sentence style is curt and choppy.

A better approach would be this one:

Dear ----------:

We've received your request to repair one of our company's vacuum cleaners, model 6983a, serial #4157831.

In reviewing our records and the sales slip shipped with the vacuum cleaner, we note that the warranty expired three months ago. For this reason, we are unable to make the repairs at the expense of the Small Appliance Manufacturing Corporation.

Accordingly, we have returned the appliance to you.

Should you wish to have the vacuum cleaner repaired at one of our authorized service centers, I've enclosed a list of such centers.

Sincerely,

The second version is better, for it (1) leads up to the "no" answer, (2) uses pronouns to add the personal touch, (3) flows smoothly from beginning to end, (4) offers help, the list of service centers, and (5) avoids accusing the customer of damaging the appliance.

In short, when writing a "no" letter, lead up to the bad news, try to be helpful, and keep a personal and friendly touch throughout.

To demonstrate some additional writing styles, let's assume that you're a personnel analyst in the headquarters office of a large corporation. To a large extent, the corporation's divisions administer their own personnel operations. From time to time, however, a division's personnel office appeals to headquarters for advice and policy. The headquarters personnel office receives this memo:

> To: Robert Jones, Chief
>   Personnel Services Branch
>   Headquarters Division
>   Multinational Corporation
>
> From: Martha Smith, Manager
>   Personnel Office
>   Continental Survey Division
>   Multinational Corporation
>
> Subject: Flight Pay for Roger Cannon
>
> Date: October 28, 1983

We are requesting permission to continue paying flight pay to a company pilot who, through no fault of his own, temporarily will do no flying.

The pilot is Roger Cannon. Mr. Cannon is an associate civil engineer in the division and is the division's helicopter pilot. His duties include flying survey teams to remote locations; once at a remote location, Mr. Cannon assists in conducting the survey.

From December 1 through January 31, the division's helicopter will be removed from service to undergo an engine change and periodic inspection and maintenance.

During those two months, Mr. Cannon will be working in the division's home office, planning the survey schedule for the next year.

Company *Personnel Actions Manual* (*PAM*), Section 201.5, authorizes the payment of $200.00 per month additional pay for persons who pilot corporate aircraft at least five hours per month. Section 201.5 does not say that pay must be discontinued in Mr. Cannon's case. In addition, the *Special Operations Pay Manual* is silent on the issue of flight pay for a helicopter pilot.

In short, there is a conflict in the manuals, and we ask that the conflict be resolved in Mr. Cannon's favor.

The branch chief hands the memo to you and asks you to research the problem and write up an analysis. You do, and you put your findings in a memo that takes this form:

To: Bob Jones

From: Your Name

Subject: Flight Pay for Roger Cannon

Date: November 7, 1983

You asked me to provide a recommendation as to whether Roger Cannon of the Continental Services Division(CSD) should continue to receive flight pay during the two months that he is not flying through no fault of his own. This request was made in an October 28, 1983, memo (attached) from CSD's personnel chief, Martha Smith.

My recommendation is no. This recommendation is based on:

1. *Special Operations Pay Manual* (June 1980, p. 11). This manual says: "When an individual vacates a posi-

tion for which special skill pay is authorized or when the position no longer requires an employee to use the special skill, the division MUST [emphasis in original] remove the employee from special skill pay status."

2. The definition of a special skill. The *Special Operations Pay Manual* (p. 3) defines a "special skill" as a "skill that requires training or experience in addition to that normally used in routine job activities." The definition includes two examples—bilingual ability and marine diving. Piloting a helicopter is not listed. Still, flying a helicopter is not normally the task of a civil engineer and, for that reason, should be considered a special skill.

3. A matter of equity. In brief, all the rest of Multinational's employees who do not fly also do not receive flight pay. Therefore, it isn't fair to these employees to make a special exception for one individual.

The style of your memo demonstrates these good features:

1. *Informal.* The memo is addressed to Bob Jones, not Robert Jones. Most intra-office business is conducted on a first-name basis these days, and there's no reason in this case to switch over to a more formal style just because the message is in writing.

2. *Personal.* The informal form of address plus the use of personal pronouns give the memo the desired personal touch.

3. *Direct.* The answer is easily seen, at the start of the second paragraph, and not buried somewhere near the bottom. Remember, this memo is not addressed to Roger Cannon. Instead, the "no" answer is for the information of your supervisor. The memo is a problem-solving one and not a true piece of commercial correspondence. If the memo were to be sent to Cannon or to Martha Smith, the "no" answer would be given *after* the facts and reasons had been presented.

4. *Forceful.* The memo does not beat around the bush. You've stated your recommendations clearly. The facts—from the *Personnel Actions Manual*—are given first and followed by your opinion on equity, and the memo contains only one conditional term, a *should* in item 2.

Notice also that the first paragraph of the memo summarizes Martha Smith's memo. This summary is a standard feature of much business correspondence. The opening summary is used to: (1) refresh the reader's memory and (2) provide continuity for later reference. An opening summary in a business letter is much like walking up to a person on the street and saying, "Remember me? I met you at the Donaldson's party last week."

Anyway, your supervisor reads your memo and agrees with your recommendation. Then he tells you to write a memo for his signature to Martha Smith. Because you're saying no to her, the memo takes this form:

> To: Martha Smith, Manager
>   Personnel Office
>   Continental Services Division
>   Multinational Corporation
>
> From: Robert Jones, Chief
>   Personnel Services Branch
>   Headquarters Division
>   Multinational Corporation
>
> Subject: Flight Pay for Roger Cannon
>
> Date: November 10, 1983

In your October 28, 1983, memo, you requested permission to continue the flight pay of Roger Cannon. Through no fault of his own, Mr. Cannon will not be piloting your division's helicopter during December and January.

Although not totally clear on this issue, the company's *Special Operations Pay Manual* can be read to provide some guidance. For instance, marine diving is referred to in the manual as a special skill that requires "training or experience in addition to that normally used in routine job activities." The same can be said for flying a helicopter. Therefore, the skill of a helicopter pilot can be considered "special" along with that of marine diver.

In addition, consideration must be given to Multinational's employees who do not receive special skill pay. To be fair to these employees, it would not be appropriate to provide special skill pay to an employee who is not using his or her special skill.

Accordingly, the policy of Multinational Corporation is that an employee not be paid flight pay unless he or she flies the minimum required five hours per month.

The stylistic attributes of this memo are:

1. *Organized as a "no" memo.* Martha Smith's division wants to pay flight pay to a respected employee, and this memo turns down the request. Therefore, leading up to the "no" answer is the proper approach.

2. *Organizational style.* "The policy of Multinational Corporation" is cited (last paragraph)—not "my policy" the "my" meaning Robert Jones's. The policy is an organizational one and should be stated as such. Because of this Robert Jones stays in the background and is firm in his choice of words. He does not say *"I* believe," but "consideration *must* be given." He does not write "in *my* opinion," but "it would *not* be appropriate."

3. *Clearly stated answer.* Even though the "no" answer is delayed until the last paragraph, the answer is stated in specific language: "an employee *not* be paid."

To carry this same problem one more step, let's assume

that your supervisor says, "Let's put out a policy memo on this issue to all the divisions." The policy memo takes this form:

> To: All Personnel Officers
>   Multinational Corporation
>
> From: Robert Jones, Chief
>   Personnel Services Branch
>   Headquarters Division
>   Multinational Corporation
>
> Subject: Flight Pay
>
> Date: November 16, 1983

A question has arisen concerning the payment of flight pay to a company pilot who temporarily does not pilot corporate aircraft. This question arose because *Special Operations Pay Manual* does not define piloting an aircraft as a special skill.

In this regard, the policy of the Multinational Corporation is that an employee not be paid flight pay unless he or she pilots corporate aircraft at least five hours per month.

This policy is effective December 1, 1983.

The next change to the *Special Operations Pay Manual* will contain an expanded definition of "special skill."

The style of the policy memo is:

1. *Impersonal.* A policy memo is not a personal letter or a memo to a customer or an acquaintance. The memo above is no more than an internal policy statement that must be easy to read but need not possess any special literary qualities.

2. *Vague as to origin of the problem.* No reason exists to single out Roger Cannon or the Continental Services Division; to mention them allows readers to infer that Cannon or the Continental Services Division caused the problem. Accordingly, the memo begins in vague terms: "A question has arisen." Neither does the memo limit the policy to helicopter pilots but refers instead to anyone who "pilots corporate aircraft."

3. *Concise.* An opening paragraph introduces the problem, the policy is stated, and the memo ends. That's all.

To sum up this discussion of style, we can say that the effective business writer realizes that:

- Style has an impact on the reader.
- Style depends upon the situation.

Finally, we talk of style as being a personal or organizational way of writing, but we should also realize that style reveals certain national characteristics. Much of American business writing typifies the American way of life: informal and brisk. On the other hand, Japan is a nation of polite and respectful people, and these national traits show up in letters like this:

Mr. Kaneyuki Taeshiro
International A&M

The summer heat is still lingering, but we hope that you are as prosperous as ever and we thank you very much for your constant patronage.

Concerning your request that the inquiry report be sent to you not by sea mail but by air mail and that two voucher copies be sent you immediately upon publication, we have asked Hitchcock to meet your request as you see in the enclosed copy. We shall be happy if you find it satisfactory.

It has not yet been long since I took over my duties from my predecessor and I may not be up to your expectations in many respects. But I am determined to do my very best, so please give me your further patronage and guidance.

It will be some time before autumn cool. I pray that you take good care of yourself.

Sincerely,
Kazunobu Marusugi[3]

Americans may be ready for Japanese cars, Japanese television sets, and Japanese wristwatches—but are we ready for the Japanese style of letter writing? I don't think so.

Rewrite, rewrite, rewrite

13

Advice on (1) the checklist method of rewriting and (2) rewriting by ear. *Plus* the rewriting habits of Ernest Hemingway, Robert Penn Warren, Simon Gray, and Colleen McCullough. *Ending* with a question about a penguin.

During an interview, Ernest Hemingway explained everything you need to know about rewriting:

INTERVIEWER: Do you do any rewriting as you read up to the place you left off the day before? Or does that come later, when the whole is finished?

HEMINGWAY: I always rewrite each day up to the point where I stopped. When it is all finished, naturally you go over it. You get another chance to correct and rewrite when someone else types it, and you see it clean in type. The last chance is in the proofs. You're grateful for these different chances.

INTERVIEWER: How much rewriting do you do?

HEMINGWAY: It depends. I rewrote the ending to *Farewell to Arms*, the last page of it, thirty-nine times before I was satisfied.

INTERVIEWER: Was there some technical problem there? What was it that had stumped you?

HEMINGWAY: Getting the words right.[1]

* * *

Getting the words right. That is all there is to writing and rewriting. Getting the words right. Do that and you've done your job. And rewriting is just part of the job of being a writer:

"I keep poems for months at a time before I let them go. I rework them a lot. I wouldn't want to give the impression that I dash off some poem a day."—Pulitzer Prize winner Robert Penn Warren.[2]

"I generally start [a play] with somebody saying something, and then hope that somebody else will say something in reply. Twenty-five drafts later there may be a play."—playwright Simon Gray.[3]

The Thorn Birds, Colleen McCullough's first best-selling book, was the product of ten drafts. Her second bestseller, *Indecent Obsession,* was the product of thirteen drafts.[4]

Just how do you go about getting the words right? In answer to that question, I'm going to recommend two methods, to be used together. The first relies on a checklist and requires you to question and challenge your writing. The second is a little more artistic and requires you to judge how well your writing sounds.

A REWRITER'S CHECKLIST

Good writers are aware of the need to rewrite. They have trained themselves to spot and correct weak points in their drafts. The techniques vary. Some writers, under the pressure of deadlines, rewrite as they go along. Others have the luxury of putting drafts away overnight or a few days until the rewriting can be done with a fresh attitude. Some need only one trip through a draft to make the needed corrections. Others go through again and again—checking, correcting, refining, and polishing.

Regardless of technique, the effective rewriter is one

who follows this basic rule: *Challenge everything on the page.* The challenging is done by asking question after question, and the questions can be arranged like a checklist into four areas: material, organization, style, and mechanics.

Material. Most first drafts do not contain enough information. Ideas are not fully developed, and not enough details are provided to inform or interest readers. Therefore, two questions that can be asked in this area are:

• Should more examples and explanations be provided?
• Do the facts need more interpretation?

It is also helpful to take the "so what" approach. That is, stop at the end of every sentence and ask:

• *So what?*
• What does this mean to the reader?
• What words or terms in this sentence must be explained before I go on?

Another question is one that many professional writers use as a guiding principle. It is a question that was stated earlier in this book and is worth repeating here.

• What does my reader *need* to know?

Organization. The final version must be organized to serve the reader. Overall organization can be challenged by asking:

• Can readers quickly find important items, or does the writing resemble a mystery story?

Internal organization can be checked by attacking each paragraph with these questions:

- Does each paragraph begin with a topic sentence?
- Is each paragraph limited to a single topic?
- Does one paragraph logically lead to the next, and is the connection obvious?
- Are the gaps filled in?

Style. Style can be strengthened by asking questions about sentences and words:

- Does any sentence sound clumsy when read aloud?
- Are sentences too long?
- Are sentences too slow in getting to the point?
- Do sentences contain interrupting elements that break up the flow of thought?
- Is the word choice suitable for the audience?
- Is each word used correctly?
- Does the text contain any jargon that should be put into plain English?
- Are excess words deleted?

Mechanics. Capitalization, grammar, punctuation, spelling, and the use of numerals must be checked. Common problems can be resolved by asking:

- Does each pronoun refer to the correct noun?
- Do verbs and nouns agree in number—singular to singular, plural to plural?
- Is the writing consistent in the way that numerals and capital letters are used?
- Are spelling and punctuation correct?

HOW DOES IT SOUND?

After you've written, and rewritten, and rewritten, and rewritten again, the next step is to read your writing out loud, while asking: How does it sound?

Are there any "breathtaking" sentences? A long sentence is not always obvious on paper. Reading a long sentence aloud, however, is something else:

> Nevertheless, and for the worst case, assuming the combustion of sulfur-bearing oil in all the in-line heaters anticipated in the refinery cost estimate, the increase in emissions due to the reheat of flue gases entering selective catalytic reduction systems in the South Coast Air Basin would be 38 tons of NOx per year, 231 tons of SOx per year, and 13 tons of particulate matter per year.

You have to take a deep breath before you read that sentence out loud; otherwise, you'll be shortwinded at the end. And the task of breaking it into shorter chunks is relatively easy:

> If the refinery cost estimate was calculated for the worst case, all of the in-line heaters would burn sulfur-bearing oil. This would increase emissions due to the reheat of flue gases entering selective catalytic reduction systems in the South Coast Air Basin. Under this worst-case assumption, the annual increase in emissions would be 38 tons of NOx, 231 tons of SOx, and 13 tons of particulate matter.

Reading out loud will help you detect awkward sentences like this one:

> The juror does not receive the jury duty fee for the time spent waiting for the telephone notification for jury duty is not being performed during that time.

That sentence is a little long, it uses the words *for* and *the* too much, and it needs internal punctuation. Let's add the punctuation first:

The juror does not receive the jury duty fee for the time spent waiting for the telephone notification [comma], for jury duty is not being performed during that time.

Now let's reduce the number of *for*'s and *the*'s:

The juror does not receive the jury duty fee *during* the time spent waiting for [no *the*] telephone notification, for jury duty is not being performed during that time.

So far we've added a comma, cut out one *the,* and changed a *for* to *during.* The sentence was twenty-eight words long to begin with; now it's twenty-seven. Can it be made shorter? Certainly:

The juror receives no jury duty fee while awaiting telephone notification, for jury duty is not being performed during that time.

That version is twenty-one words long. It's easier to read and to understand. You could tamper with it some more, but not much would be gained. Therefore, move on to something else.

Reading out loud can also help isolate dubious punctuation, or lack of punctuation, that might otherwise go unnoticed:

The prisoner said the witness was a convicted thief.

In that sentence, the stigma is placed on the witness. The addition of commas alters the meaning:

The prisoner, said the witness, was a convicted thief.

If you've found that problem, why not keep working and make the sentence even easier to understand?

The witness said that the prisoner was a convicted thief.

Now the reader knows who said what about whom.

Reading aloud is a good way to check *parallelism,* the principle that requires related items to be stated in similar forms. As examples:

Not parallel

1. Each division should designate a unit security officer.

2. The names of these officers should be forwarded to the Security Management Branch.

3. Remind unit security officers of their responsibilities as set forth in Headquarters Manual 201.7.

4. If you are a unit security officer, make certain you fill out and initial the daily log.

That example contains too many different approaches for the reader. The example would be easier to follow if rewritten:

Parallel

1. Each division should designate a unit security officer.

2. Each division should forward the name of its unit security officer to the Security Management Branch.

3. Each division should remind its unit security officer of the responsibilities as set forth in Headquarters Manual 201.7.

4. Each division should tell its unit security officer to fill out and initial the daily log.

What's right about the example just given? It consists of four parallel items, items in which the grammatical constructions are the same. Parallelism makes this version easier to read than its predecessor.

But what's wrong with it? Your ear will tell you. Each sentence begins with: "Each division should." Faults like that are fixed by writing the common phrase once and using it as a lead-in to the other items:

Each division should:
1. Designate a unit security officer.
2. Forward the name of its unit security officer to the Security Management Branch.
3. Remind its unit security officer of the responsibilities set forth in Headquarters Manual 201.7.
4. Tell its unit security officer to fill out and initial the daily log.

This final version is briefer than the original and consists of four parallel elements. These attributes make for easy reading. Notice also how each element begins with good, active verbs—*designate, forward, remind,* and *tell*—verbs that lend strength to writing and carry the reader along.

The sound of good writing is also the sound of variety. That is, sentences should not all be of the same length and of the same style. To make them so lulls readers to sleep. Consider this paragraph, which I've changed slightly from its original form:

It is a little known fact that streams were polluted even before the advent of industry and agriculture. Early travelers through Great Plains States like Nebraska had difficulty in finding clean water to drink because of wild buffalo. These animals liked to congregate in rivers where they could drink, cool off, and smear themselves with mud to ward off the hordes of gnats, flies, and other biting insects. As they spent much of their time in the water and at the water's edge, the lakes, rivers, and streams used by them became polluted with animal waste. In Nebraska, the Pawnee Indians once called one of the rivers, "Buffalo Manure Creek."

Basically, that's a well-written paragraph. It's easy to read and it's informative. But the original version was better:

It is a little known fact that streams were polluted even before the advent of industry and agriculture. Early travelers through Great Plains States like Nebraska had difficulty in finding clean water to drink. The reason: wild buffalo. These animals liked to congregate in rivers where they could drink, cool off, and smear themselves with mud to ward off the hordes of gnats, flies, and other biting insects. As they spent much of their time in the water and at the water's edge, the lakes, rivers, and streams used by them became polluted with animal waste. In Nebraska, the Pawnee Indians once called one of the rivers, "Buffalo Manure Creek."[5]

Notice the four-word sentence "The reason: wild buffalo." It provides a pleasant jolt and emphasizes a key point. This simple device adds a variety not found in the version I tampered with.

This chapter ends with the story of the youngster who asked, "Dad, what's a penguin?" The father replied, "I think it's some sort of arctic bird, but ask your mother." After some thought, the child responded, "No. I don't want to learn that much."

If by now you haven't learned more than you care to about business writing, then look in the appendix for some handy sources of further information.

Further reading and reference

DICTIONARIES

The American Heritage Dictionary of the English Language. New College Edition. Boston: Houghton Mifflin Company, 1981.

Illustrated; includes advice on word usage.

Oxford American Dictionary. New York: Oxford University, 1980.

The careful use of graphic devices and different typefaces make this dictionary very easy to use.

Webster's New Collegiate Dictionary. Springfield, Massachusetts: G.&C. Merriam Company, 1983.

Updated frequently; an excellent desk dictionary; shows the year a word was first used.

Webster's New World Dictionary of the American Language. Second college edition. New York: William Collins + World Publishing Co., 1980.

Stresses American usage.

If you have the money to spare and a need for something bigger than a desk dictionary, two recommended works are:

The Random House Dictionary of the English Language. New York: Random House, 1966.

Contains 260,000 entries and 2,000 illustrations; dictionaries of French, German, Italian, and Spanish; and a variety of useful appendixes.

Webster's Third New International Dictionary of the English Language. Springfield, Massachusetts: G.&C. Merriam Company, 1981.

Contains 460,000 entries and 3,000 illustrations. An excellent reference work.

GRAMMAR, PUNCTUATION, STYLE, AND WORD USAGE

The Associated Press Stylebook and Libel Manual. New York: The Associated Press, 1982.

Alphabetically arranged. Good on the style followed by newspapers. If the *Associated Press Stylebook* is not available, you might try a similar book, *The New York Times Manual of Style and Usage.*

Follet, Wilson, and others. *Modern American Usage: A Guide.* New York: Hill and Wang, 1966.

Alphabetically arranged. Good for style and word usage.

Fowler, H. W. *A Dictionary of Modern English Usage.* Second edition. New York: Oxford University Press, 1965.

Alphabetically arranged. Exhaustive advice on choosing the right word.

Gowers, Sir Ernest. *The Complete Plain Words.* Revised ed. London: Her Majesty's Stationery Office, 1973.

Although directed to English civil servants, *The Complete Plain Words* offers excellent guidance to any writer.

Strunk, William, Jr., and White, E.B. *The Elements of Style.* Third edition. New York: Macmillan Publishing Co., 1979.

For the advanced writer, *The Elements of Style* is the classical guidebook.

Turabian, Kate L. *A Manual for Writers of Term Papers, Theses, and Dissertations.* Fourth edition. Chicago: The University of Chicago Press, 1973.

A good, brief guide to the form of punctuation, numerals, capitalization, footnotes, bibliographies, and more.

The University of Chicago Press. *The Chicago Manual of Style.* Thirteenth edition. Chicago: The University of Chicago Press, 1982.

The editor's bible. Thorough instructions on the form of punctuation, footnotes, bibliographies, capitalization, numerals, tables, illustrations, indexes, and more.

WRITING ABOUT THE LAW IN PLAIN LANGUAGE

Flesch, Rudolf. *How to Write Plain English: A Book for Lawyers and Consumers.* New York: Harper & Row, 1979.

For forty years, Rudolf Flesch has been writing books that tell us how to write clearly. *How to Write Plain English: A Book for Lawyers and Consumers* is one of his most recent works on the subject.

Mellinkoff, David. *Legal Writing: Sense and Nonsense.* St. Paul, Minnesota: West Publishing, 1982.

Mellinkoff is a lawyer and an authority on the language of the law. *Legal Writing* is a collection of rules and samples for converting legalese to plain English.

Redish, Janice C. "How to Write Regulations (and Other Legal Documents) in Clear English." *Legal Notes and Viewpoints Quarterly,* August 1981.

Offers practical advice and good samples.

Wydick, Richard C. *Plain English for Lawyers.* Durham, North Carolina: Carolina Academic Press, 1979.

Wydick is a professor of law at the University of California, Davis. *Plain English for Lawyers* offers concise, accurate, and easy-to-read guidance.

Chapter notes

Introduction

1. William Strunk, Jr., and E. B. White, *The Elements of Style,* 3rd ed. (New York: Macmillan Publishing Co., 1979), p. 66.

1. Care for Your Reader

1. "The Practical Writer," *The Royal Bank Letter,* January/February 1981, p. 1.
2. Don Novello, *The Lazlo Letters* (New York: Workman Publishing Company, 1977).
3. Daniel B. Felker and others, *Guidelines for Document Designers* (Washington, D.C.: American Institutes for Research, November 1981), p. 33.

Note: Guidelines for Document Designers and *Document Design: A Review of the Relevant Research,* both cited here, summarize research performed by a number of scholars.

4. Janice C. Redish, "How to Write Regulations (And Other Legal Documents) in Clear English," *Legal Notes and Viewpoints Quarterly,* August 1981, p. 83.
5. Reported by Herb Caen, in the *San Francisco Chronicle,* January 19, 1979, p. 25.
6. Marlin C. Young, "Four Problems Relating to Awareness of Metacommunication in Business Correspondence," *The Journal of Business Communication,* Fall 1978, pp. 39–47.
7. Morris L. West, "How to Write a Novel," *The Writer,* May 1977, p. 9.

2. Treat Words and Meanings with Respect

1. Lester Brooks, *Behind Japan's Surrender: The Secret Struggle That Ended an Empire* (New York: McGraw-Hill Book Co., 1968), pp. 160–72; Robert J. C. Butow, *Japan's Decision to Surrender* (Stanford, California: Stanford University Press, 1954), pp. 142–65; William J. Coughlin, "The Great *Mokusatsu* Mistake," *Harper's Magazine*, March 1953, pp. 31–40; Toshikazu Kase, *Journey to the Missouri* (New Haven, Connecticut: Yale University Press, 1950), pp. 207–11; Takenobu Yoshitaro, ed., *Kenkyusha's New Japanese-English Dictionary* (1939; reprint, Cambridge, Massachusetts: Harvard University Press, 1942), p. 1256.
2. Charlton Laird, *The Word: A Look at the Vocabulary of English* (New York: Simon and Schuster, 1981), p. 184.
3. Bertram Raphael, "The Handling of Natural Language by a Computer," *Computers and People,* September 1976, p. 9.

3. Be Specific

1. John D. Bransford and Marcia K. Johnson, "Consideration of Some Problems in Comprehension," in William G. Chase, ed., *Visual Information Processing* (New York: Academic Press, 1973), p. 400.
2. Mark Twain, *Life on the Mississippi* (New York: New American Library, 1961), p. 120.
3. William F. Cox, Jr., "Problem Solving as a Function of Abstract or Concrete Words," *Contemporary Educational Psychology* 3, (1978):95–101; Daniel B. Felker, ed., *Document Design: A Review of the Relevant Research* (Washington, D.C.: American Institutes for Research, April 1980), p. 9.
4. Robert M. Pirsig, *Zen and the Art of Motorcycle Maintenance* (New York: Bantam Books, 1974), pp. 24–5.

5. Ernest Hemingway, *The Old Man and the Sea* (New York: Charles Scribner's Sons, 1952), pp. 9–10.
6. Chris John Amorosino, "Effective Communication: The Throat You Save May be Your Own," *IABC Journal* 4 (1982):13.
7. A. J. Barker, *The Vainglorious War 1854–56* (London: Weidenfeld and Nicolson, 1970), pp. 163–4.
8. Philip Warner, *The Crimean War* (London: Arthur Baker Limited, 1972), p. 70.
9. Alfred, Lord Tennyson, "The Charge of the Light Brigade," in Ralph L. Woods, ed., *A Treasury of the Familiar*, vol. 1 (Chicago: Spencer Press, 1942), p. 475.

4. Make Relationships Clear

1. Ambrose Bierce, *The Devil's Dictionary* (1911; reprint ed., New York: Dover Publications, Inc., 1958), p. 79.
2. John R. Baker, "English Style in Scientific Papers," *Nature*, November 5, 1955, p. 852.
3. Daniel B. Felker, ed., *Document Design: A Review of the Relevant Research* (Washington, D.C.: American Institutes for Research, April 1980), p. 10.
4. Felker, *Document Design*, p. 13.
5. Edward G. de Beaumont, "Thou Shalt Not Commit Adultery," *Editors Workshop*, May/June 1980, p. 13.

5. Be Positive

1. Daniel B. Felker, ed., *Document Design: A Review of the Relevant Research* (Washington, D.C.: American Institutes for Research, April 1980), pp. 13, 18, 122.

6. VERBS! VERBS! VERBS!

1. R. Buckminster Fuller, "No More Secondhand God," in *No More Secondhand God and Other Writings* (Carbon-

dale, Illinois: Southern Illinois University Press, 1963), p. 28.

2. Daniel B. Felker and others, *Guidelines for Document Designers* (Washington, D.C.: American Institutes for Research, November 1981), p. 29.

3. Jane R. Walpole, "Why Must the Passive Be Damned?" *College Composition and Communication,* October 1979, p. 251.

4. *The Wall Street Journal,* April 27, 1983. The samples are from pages 1 and 2 in the order shown.

7. *Keep Shoptalk in the Shop*

1. Trent C. Root, Jr., "The Failure of Scientists to Communicate," *Vital Speeches of the Day,* December 15, 1977, p. 133.

2. Tuli Kupferberg, "An Insulting Look at Lawyers Through the Ages," *Juris Doctor,* October/November 1982, p. 62.

3. Kupferberg, "An Insulting Look at Lawyers Through the Ages."

4. Andrew A. Lypscomb, ed., *The Writings of Thomas Jefferson,* 20 vols. (Washington, D.C.: The Thomas Jefferson Memorial Association, 1904), 17:417–8.

5. Jonathan Swift, *Gulliver's Travels* (New York: Lancer Books, 1968), pp. 342–4.

6. Code of Federal Regulations, Title 36, Paragraph 50.10.

7. Palsgraf v. Long Island Railroad Co., 248 N.Y. 339, 162 N.E. 99 (1928); in Richard C. Wydick, *Plain English for Lawyers* (Durham, North Carolina: Carolina Academic Press, 1979), pp. 5–6.

8. *Use Abbreviations with Care*

1. Ellen T. Crowley, ed., *Acronyms, Initialisms, & Abbreviations Dictionary,* 7th ed., 3 vols. (Detroit, Michigan: Gale Research Company, 1980), l:vii.

2. *Brewer's Dictionary of Phrase and Fable,* p. 1
3. Crowley, *Acronyms, Initialisms, & Abbreviations Dictionary,* l:vii.
4. Robert Graves and Alan Hodge, *The Reader over Your Shoulder: A Handbook for Writers of English Prose,* 2nd. ed. (New York: Random House, 1971), p. 62.
5. "The Agonies of Acronymania," *Time,* July 20, 1970, p. 59.

9. Break Up Long Sentences

1. From a 1741 legal formbook, quoted in David Mellinkoff, *The Language of the Law* (Boston: Little, Brown and Company, 1963), pp. 185–6.

10. Write Time-saving Paragraphs

1. *Encyclopaedia Britannica,* 1980 ed., vol. 15, p. 275.
2. Union Carbide Corporation, *Equal Employment Opportunity* (Union Carbide Corporation, September 1976), p. 3.
3. William S. Sneath, *The Changing Role of the U.S. Chemical Industry in International Trade* (Union Carbide Corporation, March 2, 1978), p. 1.
4. "Commerce Sponsors Plain English Forum," *Simply Stated,* December 1982–January 1983, pp. 1–2.
5. Donald M. Fisk, Harry P. Hatry, and Richard E. Winnie, *Practical Program Evaluation for State and Local Government Officials* (Washington, D.C.: The Urban Institute, 1973), p. 7.

11. Get to the Point

1. Lane Cooper, trans., *The Rhetoric of Aristotle* (New York: D. Appleton and Company, 1932), pp. 220–41.

2. These findings are reported in: Charles N. Cofer, "A Comparison of Logical and Verbatim Learning of Prose Passages of Different Lengths," *The American Journal of Psychology,* January 1941, pp. 1–20; Ellen D. Gagne, "Long-term Retention of Information Following Learning from Prose," *Review of Educational Research,* Fall 1978, pp. 629–65; Bonnie J. F. Meyer, *The Organization of Prose and Its Effects on Memory* (New York: American Elsevier, 1975). The above sources report corresponding findings from studies performed as far back as 1896. Other sources consulted were: Frederick Hansen Lund, "The Psychology of Belief," *The Journal of Abnormal and Social Psychology* 20 (1925): 174–96; Wilbur Schramm, "Measuring Another Dimension of Newspaper Readership," *Journalism Quarterly,* December 1947, pp. 293–306; and Harold Sponberg, "A Study of the Relative Effectiveness of Climax and Anti-climax Order in Argumentative Speech," *Speech Monographs* 13 (1946): 35–44.

3. Renée Y. Magid, *Child Care Initiatives for Working Parents: Why Employers Get Involved* (New York: American Management Associations, 1983).

12. *Vary Your Style*

1. Bernard DeVoto, ed., *The Portable Mark Twain* (New York: The Viking Press, 1946), pp. 762–3.

2. DeVoto, *Twain,* p. 776.

3. Saburo Haneda and Hirosuke Shima, "Japanese Communication Behavior as Reflected in Letter Writing," *The Journal of Business Communication,* Winter 1982, p. 29.

13. *Rewrite, Rewrite, Rewrite*

1. George Plimpton, ed., *The Paris Review Interviews,* Second Series (New York: The Viking Press, 1963), p. 222.

2. *The Writer,* February 1981, p. 5.
3. *The Writer,* July 1981, p. 3.
4. *The Writer,* February 1982, p. 6.
5. U.S. Department of Agriculture, *Meat Research* (Washington, D.C.: U.S. Government Printing Office, January 1975), p. 70.

Index

Italic type in main entry signifies a word or expression commented on within the text.